TONGUES, HEALING,
and YOU

TONGUES, HEALING, and YOU

by
DON W. HILLIS

BAKER BOOK HOUSE
Grand Rapids, Michigan

Reprinted 1969, 1972, 1973, by
Baker Book House Company

ISBN: 0-8010-4055-8

CONTENTS

PART I

WHAT CAN TONGUES DO FOR YOU?

PART II

WHERE IS THE GIFT OF HEALING?

PART I

WHAT CAN TONGUES DO FOR YOU?

1

CONTRAST — NOT COMPARISON

THE CHURCH OF TODAY is not the church Christ means it to be. This obvious fact should give rise to some soul-searching questions in the life of every child of God. How much that is really praiseworthy can be said of the present-day church? To what extent can optimistic terms be applied to its spiritual condition?

Any comparison of the virility and power of the 1st-century church with the 20th-century church is almost ludicrous. *Contrast, not comparison is the thing most evident.* It is only realistic to confess that the church of today possesses a form of godliness but denies the power thereof (II Tim. 3:5).

Spiritual leaders are almost unanimous in their opinion that today's church fits into the framework of the Laodicean congregation of Revelation 3:15-17, "I know thy works, that thou art neither cold nor hot: I would thou wert cold or hot. So then because thou art lukewarm, and neither cold nor hot, I will spew thee out of my mouth. Because thou sayest, I am rich, and increased with goods, and have need of nothing; and knowest not that thou art wretched, and miserable, and poor, and blind, and naked."

These facts have led the man on the street to take a dim view of the church. He, with some justification, feels that it is suited only for men and women who will not face the realities of life. Nor is the church reaching the man on the street in any decisive way.

Our American youth (many Christians among them) repeatedly express the opinion that the church is no longer relevant in the world. For this reason thousands of Christian young people are turning to the professions, feeling they can accomplish more for God as lawyers, politicians, doctors, and teachers, than they can through the church.

And who today would maintain with any sense of sincerity that rivers of living water are flowing from within the church? To the modern Christian, John 7:38-39 is little more than poetic platitude, "He that believeth on me, as the scripture hath said, out of his belly shall flow rivers of living water. (But this spake he of the Spirit, which they that believe on him should receive: for the Holy Ghost was not yet given; because that Jesus was not yet glorified.)"

The church is what its people are. If the life of the average Christian can be described by such tragic adjectives as prayerless, powerless, spineless, and fruitless, then it stands to reason the church will fit into the same definition.

This is not the church Christ meant it to be. He gave His followers every assurance that their lives would be filled with power sufficient to undertake the evangelism of the world. He gave them every reason to believe that the Spirit of God in their lives would enable them to be courageous, fruitful, powerful, victorious witnesses in any circumstance. In the economy of His program there was no place for unproductive Christian experience. The rod that doesn't bud cannot be used.

The Word of God is filled with teaching that the Christian and, hence the church, is to enjoy an abundant, abounding, and overflowing life. "I am come that they might have life, and that they might have it more abundantly" (John 10:10). God is to be glorified through much fruit-bearing on the part of His children. "Herein is my Father glorified, that ye bear much fruit; so shall ye be my disciples" (John 15:8). A tree planted by rivers of water, leaves ever green, bearing fruit in season—this is a picture of the church as God means it to be (Psalm 1). Fruitfulness cannot be separated from fullness.

But somewhere along the line we have lost out. As we compare ourselves with the early church we are ashamed and humiliated. As we stand in the holy light of God's standard for us we are condemned. Our hearts cry out for deliverance from profession without possession, from a cold formalism or ritualistic legalism which goes through motions but lacks the warm contagion of the first love.

The general apostasy of the church from the Person of Christ and the power of God is both deep and wide. We need revival, whatever that may mean.

We need a new relationship with and obedience to the blessed Holy Spirit. He must no longer remain just a doctrine in our theology. He must become the personal Administrator in our lives. And how can this be brought to pass?

11

Some would say the solution lies in turning our attention to supernatural signs. They suggest that a revival of miracles, healing, and tongues will provide the answer. Nor can we deny that the Lord granted signs and wonders to be done by the hands of the apostles. He confirmed the ministry of Paul "through mighty signs and wonders, by the power of the Spirit of God" (Rom. 15:19).

On the other hand, we are reminded of those who came to Jesus and said, "Master, we would see a sign from thee." Our Lord's reply to them was devastating—"An evil and adulterous generation seeketh after a sign" (Matt. 12:38-39). On another occasion Jesus rebuked unbelief by these words, "Except ye see signs and wonders, ye will not believe" (John 4:48).

"The Jews require a sign, and the Greeks seek after wisdom: but we preach Christ crucified," says the Apostle Paul. The obvious meaning of such a statement is that the answer to the world's needs lies neither in signs nor worldly wisdom. (Note I Cor. 2.)

Nor must we forget that signs and miracles can be wrought by the enemy. This was true in Moses' day. The Scripture warns us that "there shall arise false Christs, and false prophets, and shall show great signs and wonders; insomuch that, if it were possible, they shall deceive the very elect" (Matt. 24:24). We know that the coming of the wicked one will be with "all power and signs and lying wonders" (II Thess. 2:9).

These truths in no wise indicate that we should be wary of or avoid any ministry of the Spirit of God in our lives. They simply tell us that when

12

it comes to signs and wonders we need to be discerning and prayerful,

But are we not told to seek the gifts of the Spirit? And do these not include miracles, healing, and diversities of tongues? Indeed, and we *No* would be remiss if we sought anything less than all that the Spirit of God desires to give us. It is in this train of thought that we shall pursue our studies.

2

" 'PENTECOST' IS NOT A DENOMINATION — IT IS AN EXPERIENCE"

THE 20TH-CENTURY Pentecostal movement began in the year 1906. During the 50-odd years since its inauguration, it has grown to worldwide proportions. Under such names as Foursquare, Pentecostal, Church of God, Assemblies of God, etc., the Pentecostal movement has become the fastest growing Protestant church in the Western hemisphere.

According to *Time* magazine of November 2, 1962, Pentecostals now "outnumber traditional Protestants by at least four-to-one in most Latin American countries. Pentecostals claim one and one-half million members in Brazil. In Chile 700,000 of the country's 835,000 Protestants belong to Pentecostal churches." These are facts which deserve our studied attention.

In the light of the coldness of the mainstream of Protestantism are there lessons which we should learn from the Pentecostal movement? Is there an evangelistic zeal which could be ours if we would move in the direction of Pentecostalism?

"More and more traditional Protestants and Catholics are acknowledging a similarity between the unsophisticated, unfashionable Pentecostals and the unsophisticated, unfashionable early

Christians," says *Time* magazine. The evidence of this is seen in the following paragraphs.

There is no more significant phenomenon in the church today than the calculated attempt of old-line denominations to rediscover the Person and work of the Holy Spirit. There is an increasing stream of testimony coming from Lutheran, Episcopal, Dutch Reformed, Presbyterian, Methodist, and Baptist groups as to their experiences with regard to speaking in tongues and healing.

A recent Religious News Service release says, "About two dozen pastors and several hundred laymen of the American Lutheran church have reported 'speaking in tongues' experiences. A denominational commission is now studying these reported manifestations of the Holy Spirit's power according to an article in the *Lutheran Standard* published in Minneapolis."

The Evangelical Press Association in reporting on the same article says, "When a Christian speaks in tongues, he makes ecstatic utterances that cannot be identified as human language, except through the gift of interpretation.

"This 'spiritual speaking' termed by theologians 'glossolalia' goes back to the day of Pentecost when, according to Acts 2:4, the early Christians 'began to speak with other tongues' when they were 'filled with the Holy Ghost.' "

One writer, commenting on the growth of the phenomenon says, "It may interest you to note that within a diameter of 25 miles there are three Lutheran pastors and three Methodist pastors besides many others in the denominational churches who minister through the gifts of the Spirit, including 'speaking in tongues.' It is quite evident in our day that God is trying to reveal to us that 'Pentecost' is not a denomination—it is an experience."

AMERICAN LUTHERAN CHURCH

The Rev. Louis Holm who wrote the *Lutheran Standard* article states that the American Lutheran Church evangelism office has received letters from 11 states telling of "tongues" experiences.

Dr. Fredrik A. Schiotz, president of the American Lutheran Church, says, "The American Lutheran church is a part of the church of Jesus Christ and as such it welcomes the exercise of any gift the Holy Ghost may bestow on the believer. But the church would also be remiss if it did not remind its members that 'speaking in tongues' is one of the lesser gifts."

REFORMED CHURCH

An article appearing in the *Church Herald* (Reformed Church in America) says there are those within the communion of the Reformed Church who believe they have received from God the gift of tongues.

EPISCOPAL CHURCH

Let us look for a moment at those things which are taking place in St. Paul's Cathedral, Detroit. This is the central church of the Episcopal diocese of Michigan. It is the seat of the bishop with offices of the diocese and the church located in the adjoining diocesan-Cathedral center.

Dolores J. Priebe writes the following report after a visit to St. Paul's: "When I heard glossolalia (speaking in tongues) at the Wednesday night Bible study and prayer meeting in St. Paul's Cathedral church, Detroit, Michigan, recently, I could hardly believe my ears!

"Here was a dignified Episcopal priest, Dean Weaver, in traditional dress and background, praying for the sick and laying hands on people to receive the Holy Ghost. Occasionally he would speak in tongues and later he closed by making the sign of the cross in the name of the Father, and the Son, and the Holy Ghost!

"Dean Weaver is mature and silver-haired. His young and attractive wife was one of the lay members who was helping him to pray that the Holy Spirit would fall upon those kneeling. When he spoke, he was so informal but still eloquent. He referred to the Pentecostal experience and he had people testify about receiving the Spirit and, also, to healings. It was thrilling, and I sat there amazed!"

There is, perhaps, no one in the Episcopal church who has given more impetus to a rediscovery of the Person and work of the Holy Spirit than Father Dennis Bennett. Through the inspiration of his life and testimony several other Episcopal churches are holding "healing and speaking in tongues" meetings.

CONGREGATIONAL CHURCH

The Rev. Charles M. C. Kwock, who is pastor of the First Chinese Church of Christ in Hawaii

(Congregational), makes this statement: "Upon seeing the peace and joy written on the faces of so many of our members, as they sing in the Spirit and praise the Lord with a supernatural tongue, until 11:00 and 12:00 at night, I know that the Holy Spirit is really moving in our midst, working His wondrous miracle amongst us all."

How can one best evaluate this movement within these churches? It would certainly be a mistake to give anything less than sympathetic and studied attention to it. There must be some explanation back of the obvious hunger for God which is seen therein. We are prepared to rejoice in anything that proves to be of God.

Any conclusions, pro or con, in relation to such experiences must be reached only on the basis of "what saith the Scriptures." We will, therefore, postpone judgment until we have made a study of the Word.

In the meantime we make no mistake in asking a few questions. Is it not possible that the religious CLIMATE found in ritualistic churches gives rise to a hunger for some new religious experience? What are these tongues and healing meetings contributing to the spiritual growth of individuals and to the edification of the Body of Christ? Is it likely that prayer and Bible study sessions would accomplish more in the lives of the saints than tongues and healing meetings?

3

A LUTHERAN VOICE
SPEAKS IN TONGUES

IN THIS CHAPTER it is our desire to look carefully and sympathetically at the testimony of a Lutheran pastor. Like many of the rest of us, this servant of the Lord was concerned about the disparity between the power of the early church and lack of power in the modern church.

In considering this testimony, we are aware that doctrines are not built upon the foundations of testimonies or illustrations. However, an objective analysis of another man's experience is often profitable.

This pastor says, "The first answer to my uneasiness came through learning about the revival of the ministry of healing within the Episcopal church. Later I attended a healing mission in Christ Episcopal church in St. Paul, Minnesota.

"At a clinic for pastoral care in December, 1960, I discovered that a number of people involved in the ministry of healing were also experiencing some of the other manifestations of the Spirit described by St. Paul in I Corinthians 12.

"I wasn't eager about speaking in tongues and I didn't see any purpose in it. Then I found that old uneasiness began to stir inside me again. So I laid the matter before the Lord in prayer and said, 'Lord, if this is something you want me to have, then show me—in Your own way, in Your own time!'

"The Lord's answer came in a simple, unspectacular way. An elderly Norwegian lady—formerly a member of the Hauge Lutheran Synod, now a member of the Foursquare Church in San Pedro, called me one day and asked if she might invite some of my people to a revival they were having. As it turned out I was the one she was inviting. I had a free evening the following Thursday and decided it would be good relaxation to hear somebody else preach for a change!"

He then tells of his experience of speaking with the Pentecostal evangelist at the close of the service and of asking for the prayers of the evangelist and her husband. The three prayed together but without apparent result.

His testimony continues, "That night, sometime after midnight, I woke from a light sleep, sat bolt upright in bed and found an 'unknown tongue' hovering on my lips. Fully aware of what I was doing, I spoke a sentence in the tongue, and promptly fell back to sleep. I woke up in the morning with a clear recollection of the experience, but thought I had dreamed it. About a month later, I casually mentioned this experience to my wife and she told me: 'Oh, you didn't dream that! I was awake! I heard you! But I just thought you were talking in your sleep!'"

Subsequently he returned to the Pentecostal meeting. When the invitation was given for those who desired prayer for the baptism of the Holy Spirit this pastor went forward. He says that as he prayed with the evangelist, "A great sense of praise and joy began to well up within me and it spilled over my lips in a 'new tongue.' It was a wonderful experience though I didn't find myself behaving any differently except that I was speaking and praying to God in a different tongue!

"In the months since then I have learned that this experience was simply the beginning, a gateway into a vast new area of spiritual possibilities! St. Paul most accurately describes my own experience when he says, 'He who speaks in an unknown tongue edifies himself' (I Cor. 14:4). I had always thought of edification strictly in the terms of the understanding but Paul says that praying in tongues does not edify the understanding: 'If I pray in a tongue my spirit prays but my mind is unfruitful' (I Cor. 14:14). Praying in tongues edifies other aspects of the person than the intellect, expressly the spirit.

"This has been my own experience as I have used this gift in my private devotions. In a way I can neither understand nor explain, praying in tongues builds up my relationship with Christ —brings me more vividly into His presence. This does not deny any praying which I have done and continue to do, with the understanding. Scripture tells us clearly that the Christian life should include both: 'I will pray with the spirit[in tongues], and I will pray with the mind also' (I Cor. 14:15).

"My experience with the baptism of the Holy Spirit began with the manifestation of tongues, which is the normal Scripture pattern wherever a special manifestation is mentioned in connection with the baptism in the Spirit—Acts 2:4; 10:46; 19:6. But this was only the beginning. Christ baptizes us in the Spirit in order to bring us into a new realm of spiritual adventure and power.

"Already Christ has begun to manifest Himself in my life through my ministry in ways He never did before. I am far more aware, sometimes deeply aware, of my own weakness, sin, and shortcomings. Things I never even thought about before suddenly feel the bite of His pruning shears. Yet I have never loved Jesus or felt His love for me more keenly. I find a new hunger for the Word, and now God's truths come up off the page.

"About a month after the baptism of the Holy Spirit, I suddenly realized I was witnessing to people about Christ in a different way than I had before. There was a freedom and a sense of reality that had not been there before—I find every aspect of my life affected by this blessing. And each new manifestation has a single common denominator: Christ at the center of it! In one way or another the baptism of the Holy Spirit serves to glorify Christ. This is the surest evidence that the entire experience is of God.

"I look to the day soon when the baptism in the Holy Spirit will be sought and received by untold thousands of Christians the world over. And it is my special hope and prayer that people in our Lutheran church—clergy and laity alike—will reach out and embrace this wonderful gift of Christ that we might become His more perfect witnesses!"

A sympathetic evaluation of this testimony leads one to the following conclusions:

First, a mutual awareness of the disparity between the power of the early church and the powerlessness of the church today.

Second, an appreciation of every experience

which has made Christ more real and the Christian life more blessed to this pastor.

Third, a question concerning his use of and understanding of "the baptism of the Holy Spirit." The Book of Acts gives to us just four illustrations of people being baptized by or in the Holy Spirit. In Acts 2 they are believing Jews; in Acts 8, Samaritan believers; in Acts 10, Gentile believers; and in Acts 19, Jews of the dispersion who had known only the baptism of John. I Corinthians 12:13 is the scriptural commentary on all of these illustrations. "For by one Spirit are we all baptized into one body, whether we be Jews or Gentiles, whether we be bond or free; and have been all made to drink into one Spirit."

Williams translates this verse, "For by one Spirit *all of us...have been* baptized into one body..." Phillips says, "For *we were all* baptized by the Spirit into one body..." The 20th Century translation reads, "For it *was* by one Spirit that *we were all* baptized to form one body...."

Though there is no record of the Corinthian Christians having any form of Pentecostal experience, yet Paul tells them they *have all been* baptized into one body. As the crucifixion and resurrection of our Lord form the historic foundation upon which Paul could write, "Moreover whom he did predestinate, them he also called; and whom he called, them he also justified: and whom he justified, them he also glorified" (Romans 8:30), so Pentecost provides the historic foundation upon which our baptism into the Body of Christ is an accomplished fact.

23

If, as some would contend, only those who have had some kind of Pentecostal experience are baptized into the Body of Christ then there are thousands of believers who are not in that Body. This is both unthinkable and unscriptural.

"The baptism of the Holy Spirit was never functional, it was organic and vital," says Dr. J. Vernon McGee. One becomes a partaker in this baptism when faith is placed in Christ. "The baptism of Romans 6:3-4 is clearly the baptism of the Spirit which places one in Christ at the time of salvation," writes Dr. Roy L. Aldrich.

There are those of the Pentecostal persuasion who use the terms "baptism" and "infilling" synonymously. This is illustrated in the following statement by the Rev. Thomas F. Zimmerman, the General Superintendent of The Assemblies of God. "There are a great number of Scripture passages which would indicate that believers do not receive the *infilling* or *baptism* in the Holy Spirit at the time of conversion." (Italics his.) It would be difficult to defend Mr. Zimmerman's simultaneous usage of the two terms.

Fourth, a rejection of the implication of his statement that "the manifestation of tongues... is the normal Scripture pattern wherever a special manifestation is mentioned in connection with the baptism in the Spirit—Acts 2:4; 10:46; 19:6."

Though this statement is technically true, it must be qualified by two facts. (A) The "tongues" of Acts 2:4; 10:46; 19:6 are not necessarily the "tongues" of I Corinthians 12 and 14. (B) If the "manifestation of tongues" is the normal accompaniment of the baptism in the Spirit, then there were hundreds of converts in the Book

24

of Acts who were never baptized in the Spirit.

Fifth, a conjecture that this pastor may be confusing an experience of "new birth" with the baptism of the Holy Spirit. All of the blessed results (love for the Word, desire to witness, etc.) of his "baptism in the Spirit" are manifest in the lives of thousands of true Christians with the exception of speaking in tongues.

It is altogether likely that there are hundreds of pastors who have never been born again. It would be most natural for them to confuse the new birth with some other spiritual experience. This may be the case with the pastor in question.

Sixth, a thankfulness to God for everything He has done in the life of this pastor and a prayer that the perfect will of God may ever be his portion.

Seventh, a conviction that "the baptism in the Spirit" does not have to be "sought and received by untold thousands the world over." There is no evidence in the Word of God that any such experience ever had to be sought by any believer. A simple return to "walking in the Spirit" will produce all of the purity and power that God desires in the Christian life.

Neither the Person nor the work of the Holy Spirit can be purchased through any effort of ours. You will recall the severe rebuke delivered to Simon (Acts 8:18-24) because he sought to buy the opportunity of ministering in the power of the Spirit. We need to beware lest our efforts toward spiritual power become attempts to make God our debtor—as if He owed us some special gifts because we have spent so much time in prayer, etc., etc.

4
LAYING A FOUNDATION

THOUGH THE OLD TESTAMENT has much to say concerning the Person and work of the Holy Spirit, we will limit ourselves to just two thought-provoking lessons which are readily seen therein.

First...The lives of such saints as Enoch, Noah, and Abraham clearly reveal that men can walk with God without any apparent theological understanding of the Person and work of the Holy Spirit. The lives of Elijah and Elisha indicate that miracles were wrought by men who themselves may have had little or no concept of the doctrine of the Trinity.

Second...Several Old Testament characters who proved themselves reprobate were on occasion filled with the Spirit for specific ministries. This is demonstrated in the lives of Balaam and Saul. These illustrations do not put a premium on ignorance of the Holy Spirit. They simply demonstrate the grace of the Third Person of the Trinity in His dealings with men. They warn us to beware of limiting what the Holy Spirit can do in another man's life.

As we move into the New Testament, we are early introduced to John the Baptist. Our Lord referred to John as the greatest prophet born of women (Luke 7:28). He is the only man in history who is spoken of as being filled with the Holy Spirit from his mother's womb (Luke 1:15). This places him in a category which demands our careful attention.

It has been estimated that the ministry of John the Baptist did not last over six months. During that time he exerted a powerful influence in a localized area. It is noteworthy that this Holy Spirit-filled man did no miracles (John 10:41). He did no healings and apparently never spoke in unknown tongues. But he lived so much like the expected Messiah that men asked him, "Art thou the Christ?"

The plain implication of this is that quality of life is the basic evidence of the fullness of the Spirit of God. Though John obviously had the prophetic gift, yet the graces of the Spirit in his life were more important than the gifts of the Spirit. The godliness of John's life filled Herod with terror and caused the multitudes to cry out, "What shall we do?" John's holy character distinguished him from the scribes, the Pharisees and the other religious leaders of his day. Holiness, humility, boldness, patience and a determination that Christ must increase, all gave eloquent testimony of John's Spirit-filled life. The fullness of the Spirit is the fullness of God, hence godliness must be the chief characteristic of the Spirit-filled life. Godliness is the distinguishing element so desperately needed in the church today.

Toward the end of our Lord's ministry He informed His followers it would be expedient for Him to leave them in order that the Holy Spirit might dwell with them: "Nevertheless I tell you the truth; It is expedient for you that I go away: for if I go not away, the Comforter will not come unto you; but if I depart, I will send him unto you" (John 16:7). The obvious implication of this statement is that the Spirit of God would be in a position to do something for the believer which it was not feasible for Jesus Himself to accomplish.

Jesus was looking to that day in which the Holy Spirit would not be limited to one pair of feet with which to walk, one pair of hands with which to minister, and one pair of lips with which to speak. In the redemptive program it was necessary for the Second Person of the Trinity to be limited to one body. Once the redemptive act of the crucifixion, resurrection, and ascension was accomplished, the Third Person of the Trinity could then indwell the bodies of believers everywhere. He could walk in Chinese feet along China's pathways, speak with African lips in African languages, and minister with Japanese hands to Japanese people.

Jesus also informed His followers that through the Holy Spirit they would do "even greater works" than He had done (John 14:12). In reference to "greater works" we inevitably think of the miracles of our Lord. But one must keep in mind that Christ never wrought miracles apart from a motive. The miracle was never an end in itself. His miracles were wrought in order to introduce men to Himself. The lame were healed and the blind received their sight in order that they might know that Christ had power on earth to forgive sins. Jesus' greatest work involved the bringing of men and women to a confession of faith in Himself as the Christ. The evidence, therefore, of the greatness of our works rests in the lives of men and women we bring to Him.

The basis of these "greater works" is found in

the statement, "because I go unto my Father." This was a reference to the coming of the Holy Spirit. It is He alone Who, through us, can do the greater works of revealing the truth to darkened minds and bring hearts under the conviction of sin: "And when he is come, he will be-prove the world of sin, and of righteousness, and of judgment: Of sin, because they believe not on me; Of righteousness, because I go to my Father, and ye see me no more; Of judgment, because the prince of this world is judged" (John 16:8-11).

It is evident in our Lord's teachings in John chapters 13 through 16 that the Holy Spirit is to be to us all that Christ was to His disciples . . . and more! He was their teacher. All they knew of truth they learned from Him. He was their guide. Their lives were directed according to His instructions. Above all, He was their God. Nor was He satisfied with His relationship with them until they could say, "My Lord and my God."

In like manner the Holy Spirit dwells within us as our teacher. Spiritual truth can be received through no one else than the Holy Spirit (I Cor. 2:7-14). There will never be a time in our lives in which He will not have yet many things to say unto us (John 16:12). He is, also, our guide (John 16:13; Rom. 8:14). We maintain our relationship in the center of God's will only and as we "walk in the Spirit." The will of the Holy Spirit in our lives is fulfilled in the measure in which Christ is given the place of Lordship. The epitome of the Spirit's desire for us is that we may be able to testify—"for to me to live is Christ."

5

THE BIBLE'S UNTOLD THOUSANDS WHO NEVER SPOKE IN TONGUES

BECAUSE THE BOOK OF ACTS forms the foundation upon which Pentecostal movements are built, it is imperative that we study it. We must remember, however, that Acts is not basically a book of doctrine—it is history. It can be dangerous to build doctrines from history.

In this consideration of the work of the Spirit as recorded in Acts we will primarily investigate the subject of "tongues."

It is noteworthy that the Pentecostal experience as described in Acts chapter two does not give us an illustration of speaking in "unknown tongues," i.e. ecstatic utterances. We are told that the 120 (it would be interesting to know why the several hundred other followers of Christ were not included in this upper room experience) in the upper room were "all filled with the Holy Ghost, and began to speak with *other* tongues, as the Spirit gave them utterance" (Acts 2:4). These *other* tongues were not *unknown* tongues. The Scripture is its own commentary as to what they were. In Acts 2:8 we read, "And how hear we every man in *our own tongue*, wherein we were born?" In 2:11 we read, "We do hear them speak *in our tongues* the wonderful works of God."

These other tongues were contemporary languages. It is, therefore, a misappropriation of Scripture to use the second chapter of Acts as a basis for speaking in "unknown tongues" in the sense of those tongues being ecstatic utterances not understood by men.

It should here be called to the attention of the reader that there is no place in the original in which the word "unknown" is used in reference to tongues. The translation of the King James Version supplied the word (hence it is always in italics) to distinguish the gift of ecstatic utterance from normal speech. True to the Greek, later translations omit the word "unknown."

It is, also, a mistake to consider the second chapter of Acts as a basis for "tarrying meetings." The Holy Spirit did not come upon those who were gathered in the upper room because of their tarrying. We read in Acts 2:1, "And when Pentecost *was fully come*, they were all with one accord in one place." In the sovereign wisdom of God the day of Pentecost was pre-determined, even as the birth of Christ was foreordained and came to pass in the "fullness of time."

There are only two occasions in the 28 chapters of Acts in which people spoke in "tongues." These two cases are noteworthy and must be considered honestly and with an open mind. However, before doing so, let's look at those individuals and groups who were brought to Christ in the Book of Acts and concerning whom no "speaking in tongues" experience is recorded.

We are told in Acts 2:41-42, "Then they that gladly received his word were baptized: and the

31

same day there were added unto them about three thousand souls. And they continued steadfastly in the apostles' doctrine and fellowship, and in breaking of bread, and in prayers." We have no evidence that any of this group of 3,000 ever had a "speaking in tongues" experience.

In Acts 2:47 it is recorded, "And the Lord added to the church daily such as should be saved." We have no way of knowing the number of people who were brought into the church during those days. Nor is any account given as to whether any of them spoke in tongues.

In Acts 4:4 we are told that many who heard the Word of God believed, and the number of men was about 5,000. Again, we are given no record as to any filling with the Holy Spirit or speaking in tongues. Acts 6:7 says, "The word of God increased; and the number of disciples multiplied in Jerusalem greatly; and a great company of the priests were obedient to the faith." The Scripture is silent in respect to these converts having any "Pentecostal" experience.

In Acts 4:31 we read that the believers were "filled with the Holy Ghost, and they spake the word of God with boldness." In Acts 8:15-17 we are informed that the new believers in Samaria received the Holy Ghost at the time Peter and John laid hands upon them. In neither of these cases is any mention made with regard to any of the gifts of the Spirit.

When the miracle of the resurrection of Dorcas occurred in Joppa, "many believed in the Lord" (Acts 9:42). In Acts 16:34 we have the account of the conversion of the Philippian jailor and those who were gathered in his house. There is an absence of any mention of tongues in these accounts.

Pointing out that there is no mention of the impartation of "tongues" to the many thousands of believers who are included in these illustrations is not to suggest that the Spirit of God was leaving these believers ungifted. It simply implies that "speaking in tongues" was neither a required nor a particularly significant gift as far as the record in Acts is concerned.

As we consider individual conversions within the Book of Acts, we are again impressed with the number concerning whom the subject of tongues is not mentiond.

One cannot doubt the conversion of the lame man whose healing is recorded for us in the third chapter of Acts. Verse 9 of that chapter clearly reveals his conversion. We are not, however, told of any tongues experience.

In Acts six we are introduced to the seven deacons chosen by the early church. These were of "honest report and full of the Holy Ghost and wisdom." Particular mention is later made of Stephen and Philip in respect to the effective ministries they had. Nothing is recorded, however, as to any particular gift of the Spirit in their lives except that the gift of "helps" or "administration" may have been evident in their lives, thus leading to their selection as deacons. Stephen "did great wonders and miracles among the people," but no mention is made of tongues.

Barnabas, Silas, Dorcas, Lydia, Sergius Paulus, the Philippian jailer, Crispus the chief ruler of the synagogue, Apollos, Aquila and Priscilla, and

Timothy are a few of the individuals in the Book of Acts whose lives were transformed by the Gospel. The subject of "unknown tongues" is not attached to any of these names.

We are not hereby trying to prove something negative. We are endeavoring to place "tongues" in their proper perspective. We are suggesting that it is dangerous to overemphasize that concerning which the Scripture gives comparatively little space. It is human nature to desire and to magnify the dramatic. The Book of Acts successfully avoids this.

What, after all, is the picture one gains from a study of the early church? Is it that of a little band of people who distinguish themselves from the rest of the world by their experiences in speaking in unknown tongues? Or is it that of a fearless group of people who are very much in the world, though not of it—who turn the world upside down by their bold declaration of the Gospel message in languages understood by their hearers? We do well to objectively and honestly face this question.

And now let us return for a moment to the two post-Pentecostal tongues experiences recorded in Acts. The first is found in Acts 10:46 and relates to the conversion of a Gentile household. The believing Jews who accompanied Peter to the home of Cornelius were astonished (amazed) "because that on the Gentiles also was poured out the gift of the Holy Ghost. For they heard them speak with tongues and glorify God."

In both the Phillips' and Williams' translations the word "foreign" precedes the word tongues. The implication is that this experience was similar to that recorded in Acts 2 and not a demonstration of the "ecstatic utterances" of I Corinthians 12-14. Peter's Jerusalem account of this experience ("as I began to speak the Holy Ghost fell on them, *as on us* at the beginning." Acts 11:15) strengthens this implication.

In Acts 19:1-7 we have the account of twelve believers who had been baptized unto repentance but who had not heard of the Holy Spirit. Subsequent to being baptized in the name of the Lord Jesus, Paul laid his hands on them and the Holy Spirit came on them "and they spake with tongues and prophesied."

Though we cannot be dogmatic about this, it would appear likely that these twelve men did not speak in the "ecstatic utterances" of I Corinthians 12-14 but in foreign languages.

Because the accounts in Acts 2, 10 and 19 record the experience of believers who spoke in "known" languages we ought to be careful about equating them with the gift of "unknown" tongues as it is described in I Corinthians.

6

NEITHER AN EYE NOR A TONGUE

IT IS THE PLAIN TEACHING of Scripture that one is not brought into the family of God apart from the personal operation of the Holy Spirit in his own life. That which is born of the flesh is flesh (John 3:6) and can never be anything but flesh. It may be educated, cultured, or even religious flesh, but it cannot please God (Rom. 8:8). On the other hand, that which is born of the Spirit is spirit. No student of the Scriptures will, in any wise, dispute the fact that we are children of God only and as we are born of the Spirit of God. Every child of God enters into the spiritual experience of being a member of the family of God through the work of the Holy Spirit.

In Romans 8:9 we read, "Now if any man have not the Spirit of Christ, he is none of his." In I John 4:2 it is recorded, "Hereby know ye the Spirit of God: every spirit that confesseth that Jesus Christ is come in the flesh is of God." "Whosoever shall confess that Jesus is the Son of God, God dwelleth [abides] in him," says I John 4:15. "Hereby know we that we dwell [abide] in him, and he in us, because he has given us of his Spirit," says John in the 13th verse of the fourth chapter of his epistle. It is obvious that the Christian's body becomes the temple of the Holy Spirit through the new birth (I Cor. 6:19-20).

These facts lead us to the conclusion that the

gifts of the Holy Spirit are supplemental to the Person and presence of the Holy Spirit in the Christian life. In other words, we can say without fear of contradiction that the gifts are not a necessity to salvation. When this is thoroughly understood we are in a position to consider the significance of the gifts in the Christian life.

A careful reading of I Corinthians 12, 13, and 14 leads one to the conviction that in giving so much space to the subject of tongues, Paul was facing up to a problem within the Corinthian congregation. If the apostle had given an equivalent amount of space to each of the other gifts of the Spirit, I Corinthians would have been a much longer book. Why did he not do so? The answer rests in the fact that "tongues" is a gift which can be misused and misappropriated. It therefore had to be safeguarded by detailed instructions. It was, in fact, already being misused in the Corinthian congregation.

There is almost unanimous agreement on the part of Bible scholars that the Holy Spirit has given and does give gifts to the members of the Body of Christ. Nor are we to be ignorant of these gifts (I Cor. 12:1). However, one should always keep the purpose of these gifts in proper perspective.

In I Corinthians 12:7 we read, "But the manifestation of the Spirit is given to every man to profit withal." Perhaps a free translation of this verse would read, "But the outward evidence of the indwelling Holy Spirit is given to each individual for the profit of the whole body." The practical application of this is simply the fact that the blessed indwelling Holy Spirit has placed some tool in the hand of each Christian for the upbuilding of every other Christian.

The significance of this "upbuilding" is emphasized in such exhortations as, "But covet earnestly the best gifts" (I Cor. 12:31). "Even so ye, forasmuch as ye are zealous of spiritual gifts, seek that ye may excel to the edifying of the church" (I Cor. 14:12). "Let all things be done unto edifying" (I Cor. 14:26). In this building program we are encouraged to seek the most profitable tool.

We acknowledge, then, that God has given gifts (tools, instruments) to the members of His body with the understanding that they are to be used for the building up of the church. Any public ministry, therefore, of any gift of the Spirit must be motivated by that purpose. "Tongues" edifies the individual—the other gifts edify the church.

In I Corinthians 12:4 we note that there are "diversities of gifts." The chapter then lists nine of them. They are the gifts of wisdom, knowledge, faith, healing, miracles, prophecy, discerning of spirits, tongues, and interpretation of tongues. In the 28th verse of this same chapter, a similar list is given in the following order: first, apostles; second, prophets; third, teachers; after that miracles, then gifts of healings, helps, governments, and diversities of tongues.

Between the first and second listing of the gifts the Apostle Paul carefully and emphatically illustrates the relationships of these gifts by using the human body as an analogy. He says, "For as the body is one and hath many members and all of the members of that one body being many are

38

one body so also is Christ" (I Cor. 12:12). He then proceeds to point out the fact that the various members of the body are interdependent upon one another. No organ of the body is independent of the body as a whole. Furthermore, each organ has a responsibility to each other member of the body. No single organ of the body stands as ultimate proof that the body is either alive or healthy. The combined labors of all the organs contribute to the life and health of the body.

Obviously, some members of the physical body are more significant than others. This has little to do with their attractiveness. It is their usefulness which is significant. The foot is an illustration of an organ which in itself is not attractive. It is, however, extremely useful to the overall effectiveness of the body.

As no one member of the body can claim to be the whole body, so no single gift of the Spirit can claim to be the whole ministry of the Spirit. Nor is one gift of the Spirit given to every member of the body of Christ any more than the faculty of seeing is given to every organ of the physical body. No single gift of the Spirit is for everyone. All are not apostles. All are not prophets. All are not teachers. All are not workers of miracles. Much less then do all speak with tongues or all have the gift of interpretation (I Cor. 12:29-30).

It is important to remember that the gifts of the Spirit are "gifts." One does not dictate to another when, how, or what gifts he is to receive. Gifts are given whenever, however, whyever, and to whomever at the discretion of the giver.

The Apostle strongly emphasizes this point. First he tells us that the diversity of gifts has been made by God Himself. The Spirit of God is sovereign in the number and kind of gifts He has chosen (I Cor. 12:4-6).

It is also clear that the Holy Spirit is sovereign in the distribution of those gifts, "dividing to every man severally as he will" (I Cor. 12:11). Just as Almighty God has "set the members every one of them in the body, as it hath pleased him" (I Cor. 12:18), so His omniscience is active in the distributing of the gifts to the body of Christ.

What monstrosities we would have made of our physical bodies if the arrangements of the various organs had been left to us! Certainly then the arrangement of the organs of the body of Christ cannot be left to the whims of finite minds. Can we not, and must we not, leave the distribution of His gifts in His hands?

The consistent and final counsel to us is simply to covet earnestly the best gifts. In the meantime, let us be thankful that the whole body is neither an eye nor a tongue.

7

FACING THE FACTS

THE SILENCE of most of the New Testament writers concerning the topic of "tongues" is not without significance. Though these writers give a great deal of space to the subject of the Person and work of the Holy Spirit they have nothing to say about tongues. This is true of the three epistles of John and Revelation, of the two Epistles of Peter, of James, and of Jude. It is true of Galatians, Ephesians, Philippians, Colossians, and all the rest of Paul's epistles with the exception of I Corinthians.

In contrasting the great amount of teaching given in the epistles concerning the Person and work of the Holy Spirit with the small amount of space given to tongues, one is left with an impression of the relative unimportance of tongues. One is also led to the conviction that God is more concerned about what He can do in us than what we can do for Him. In other words, because Christian character forms the foundation of service for God, it is more significant than service. The Spirit of God has no greater purpose in our lives than to conform us to the image of Christ. That "image" will reveal the "fruit of the Spirit... love, joy, peace, longsuffering, gentleness, goodness, faith, meekness, temperance."

It would be folly to give a set of carpenter's tools to a man who has no time, training, knack, or desire for carpentry. Until he has these, the tools will either rust or be misused. Nor is it the chief concern of the Spirit of God to hand out tools to His people. His first desire has to do with what we are, not with what we can do. He then places into our hands, according to His own sovereign choice, that gift which will make us most effective in edifying (building) the church.

Nor can it be said that any particular "tool" of the Spirit is the final or only conclusive evidence that a person is filled with the Spirit. It would be quite as narrow to say the only proof that a man is a builder is that he carries a hammer. The architect's pencil, the plumber's wrench, the electrician's pliers, and the mason's trowel also give testimony to the "spirit of a builder" within the lives of those who use them.

Though we cannot go into a detailed study of the Person and work of the Holy Spirit as it is given to us in the epistles, we must not overlook certain aspects which directly touch our theme.

In Ephesians 5:18 we read, "but be filled with the Spirit." The context suggests three things: One, being filled with the Spirit is a process. Two, the fullness of the Spirit is evidenced by the control and authority of the Spirit over the life. These first two factors are seen in the opening portion of the verse—"and be not drunk with wine, wherein is excess but. . ." Becoming drunk is a process which continues only as long as one continues to drink. It leads to being controlled by the "spirits" consumed, and the drunkard begins to walk in the spirit of drunkenness.

On the positive side of the picture, we are intro-

42

duced to a third point. The behavior of the Spirit- *3.*
filled life is described in Ephesians 5:19 to 6:19.
That walk which is under the control of the Holy
Spirit is one in which there is singing and making
melody in the heart to the Lord, the giving of
thanks for all things, the submitting of ourselves
one to another in the fear of the Lord, love between husband and wife, obedience of children
to parents, mutual consideration between manage-
ment and labor, victory in the face of spiritual
conflict, and prayer and supplication in the
Spirit for all saints.

The command to be filled with the Spirit stands
in contrast to the order, "and grieve not the Holy
Spirit of God" (Eph. 4:30). And how are we
to understand this order? Again it is the context
which gives us the clue. Immediately preceding
this verse we have the following instructions:
don't let the sun go down on your wrath, don't
give place to the devil, don't steal, and don't let
any corrupt communication proceed out of your
mouth. Then in the concluding two verses of the
chapter we read, "Let all bitterness, and wrath,
and anger, and clamour, and evil speaking, be put
away from you, with all malice: And be ye kind
one to another, tenderhearted, forgiving one another, even as God for Christ's sake hath for-
given you."

It is obvious from this passage that we grieve
the indwelling Holy Spirit by acts of sin...by
the unrighteous things we do, say, and think.
However, true holiness is something more than
the avoiding of unholiness. The full-orbed life
into which the Holy Spirit desires to lead us is

filled with positive demonstrations of goodness. These are possible only and as we "quench not the Spirit" (I Thess. 5:19).

We grieve the Spirit of God by the things we do. We quench the Spirit of God by the things we refuse to let Him do. He indwells us for several well-defined reasons. He desires to reveal Christ to us and through us. He is the Spirit of Truth. As such, He yearns to open the Scriptures unto us. We quench (confine) this ministry of His by refusing to expose ourselves to the Word of God.

It is the nature of the Spirit of God to speak of the things of Christ. It is His purpose to glorify Christ through spoken testimony. Any refusal on our part to be His witnesses via the spoken word is to quench (smother) His ministry.

He is also the Spirit of intercession. He is the Author of all true prayer. It is for this reason we are exhorted to pray in the Spirit. Any refusal on our part to allow Him liberty in this ministry of prayer and supplication is to quench the Spirit. Prayerlessness in our lives bears irrefutable testimony to the fact that we have quenched (shackled) the Person and work of the blessed Holy Spirit in our lives.

The Third Person of the Trinity is also the Spirit of unity. It is His nature to love the brethren. It is through Him the love of God is shed abroad in our hearts. Any lack of love on our part for the brethren, any "party" spirit, ("I am of Apollos," etc.), any spirit of divisiveness is not of Him. Any such spirit within us serves to quench the Spirit.

The children of Israel were accused of limiting

"the Holy One of Israel" (Ps. 78:41). Nor is the church any less guilty of limiting (quenching) the Person and work of the Holy Spirit. The Spirit of God is "straitened" within us. His ministry is unlimited, unhampered, and unquenched only as we walk in obedience to Him. The fullness of the Spirit is enjoyed by those who are responsive to Him. The liberty of the Holy Spirit to freely direct and control our lives, to fulfill His own wishes, and to do to us and through us all He desires is the need of the hour. *Quench not the Spirit.* There is no gift of the Spirit which can be considered a substitute for the Spirit-controlled life.

Acknowledging this fact, we are still in a position where we must honestly face some clear Bible statements concerning tongues. I refer to I Cor. 14:5, "I would that ye all spake with tongues . . ."; I Cor. 14:18, "I thank my God, I speak with tongues more than ye all:"; and I Cor. 14:39, "Forbid not to speak with tongues."

What are we to do with such declarations? We have no right to dispensationalize them out of existence. On the contrary, we gladly accept them just as we accept the teaching of the Word of God in respect to the other gifts of the Spirit. We accept these statements in the light of their contexts. It is noteworthy that the Spirit of God has surrounded each of these declarations with strong qualifying statements.

Paul's expressed desire that all might speak with tongues is immediately qualified by, "but rather that ye prophesied: for greater is he that prophesieth than he that speaketh with tongues,

45

except he interpret, that the church may receive edifying." This is not the only time in which Paul has contrasted the relative unimportance of tongues to the obvious importance of preaching the Word for the edification of the church. Furthermore, Paul has already told us that not *all* would speak in tongues. (Note I Cor. 12:10, 30.) Again it must be remembered that this gift (like all the rest) is imparted by God as it pleaseth Him, not to all but to whomsoever He wills.

Paul's own thankfulness that he is able to speak with tongues is followed by the statement, "Yet in the church I had rather speak five words with my understanding, that by my voice I might teach others also, than ten thousand words in an unknown tongue" (I Cor. 14:19). Such a statement would be ludicrous were it not inspired by the Holy Spirit. This strongly worded contrast places the gift of unknown tongues in a relatively unimportant position. It is always wise to place importance where God places it, and dangerous to overemphasize the relatively unimportant.

As Paul closes his treatise on unknown tongues he says, "Forbid not to speak with tongues." This too he qualifies by a preceding statement, "covet to prophesy" and a statement which follows, "let all things be done decently and in order." This closing command points back to Paul's careful instructions on the subject of tongues as given in I Corinthians chapters 12 through 14.

We must, therefore, conclude that:
  a. "Tongues" is not available for all, but for those to whom the Lord desires to give it.

b. "Tongues" is to be exercised in private, except when the gift of interpretation is present.
c. There are more important gifts to be desired than that of tongues.
d. Speaking in tongues is an exercise of worship which basically edifies the individual. This exercise should never replace worship with the understanding.

8

MAJORING IN THE MAJORS

THE PREPONDERANCE of Bible teaching concerning the Person and work of the Holy Spirit deals with something other than the gifts of the Spirit. In like manner the preponderance of our interest in the Third Person of the Trinity must go deeper and reach farther than a desire for those gifts. Our interest in His gifts must be secondary to our desire for His fellowship and fullness. To center our concern around the gifts of the Spirit is to major in the minors.

There were those in our Lord's day who were rebuked because they followed Him only for the bread they could obtain. We are in no less need of guarding our motive. Let us beware lest we stoop to the level of desiring the gifts of the Spirit more than the Giver.

"But I want to know He is at work in me. I want to see the results of His ministry through me." This desire is noble when and as it fits into the pattern of the revealed will of the Spirit of God. Let us look at a few of those things which are of major significance to the Holy Spirit.

It is the work of the Spirit to convict men of sin, righteousness and judgment (John 16:8). How very little of this is in evidence today! If conviction of sin, repentance toward God, and conversion to Christ are of basic importance to the Spirit, then a concern for such a manifestation of His ministry should be uppermost in our hearts. There is no substitute for a desire to see souls won to Christ. To covet the gifts of the Spirit apart from a compassion for lost men is to misunderstand the nature of the Holy Spirit.

"When he, the Spirit of truth, is come, he will guide you into all truth: . . . and he will show you things to come" (John 16:13). Is there any greater need today than for God's people to be Spirit-enlightened students of the Word? But where are those who search the Scriptures daily? Where is that congregation or person demonstrating a vital relationship to the Spirit of Truth by a knowledge of the Scriptures and hunger for the Word? There is no gift of the Spirit which can substitute for a working knowledge of the Scriptures. Unfortunately there are not a few who make bold claims relative to their "gifts" but who are woefully ignorant of the Word of God.

The Bible teaches that prayer and supplication constitute a significant ministry of the Third Person of the Trinity (Rom. 8:26-27; Eph. 6:18). Where are those whose lives reveal a spirit of prayer and supplication? Where are those who earnestly pursue a ministry of intercession? Where are those whose lives give place to the prayer ministry of the Spirit?

And what can we say about holiness? Are we not failing the Lord and the world most miserably in this regard? We talk much about revival but seem quite unprepared to seek the Person and power of the Spirit in producing holiness of life. Healing of body seems important to us while healing of the soul is neglected. We pray for those who are physically ill, but we are indifferent toward those who are plagued with spiritual sickness. This is not the kind of praying we find in the epistles.

The early church leaves one with the impression that holiness of life, oneness of heart, liberality of spirit, power in preaching, and fearlessness in witnessing are the chief characteristics of a Spirit-filled people. These things are consistently more a part of the work of the Holy Spirit than the gift of tongues which the 20th-century church now endeavors to obtain.

Note those things which characterized the lives of the believers who were filled with the Holy Ghost. ". . . and they were all filled with the Holy Ghost, and they spake the word of God with boldness. And the multitude of them that believed were of one heart and of one soul: neither said any of them that aught of the things which he possessed was his own; . . ." (Acts 4:31-32). Verse 31 teaches us that the first external evidence of the control of the Spirit in the lives of the believers was their bold declaration of the Word of God. Courage was evident in the ministry of the early church, and when the believers did not have courage, they asked for it. (Note Acts 4:13 and Acts 4:29.)

The lack of a courageous witness for Christ today presents an alarming symptom of spiritual anemia. Courage is a gift of the Spirit of God. It will not come without faith in and obedience to the truth that God has given unto us the Spirit of power, of love, and of a sound mind (II Tim. 1:7).

In Acts 4:32, we observe unity in those who were filled with the Holy Spirit. The verse informs us that the multitude of those who believed were of "one heart and of one soul." This fits in with the whole message of the Word of God concerning the Body of Christ. The ministry of the Spirit of God is never divisive within the realm of the true church.

It was the prayer of the Lord Jesus Christ that believers might "be one even as we [He and the Father] are one" (John 17:22). Although there are diversities of gifts and differences of administrations, there is but one Lord and one Spirit, who gives to every man individually as He wills. "For as the body is one and hath many members, and all the members of that one body, being many, are one body; so also is Christ" (I Cor. 12:12). The maintaining of the unity of the Spirit in the bond of peace should be as much an evidence of the fullness of the Spirit, in the 20th century as it was in the first.

A third principle which characterized the Spirit-filled life is expressed in these words, "neither said any of them that aught of the things which he possessed was his own" (Acts 4:32). Selfishness is natural; unselfishness is supernatural. Greed is of the flesh; liberality is of the Spirit.

The grace of liberality is exemplified in the churches of Macedonia. We are told that it was "in a great trial of affliction, the abundance of their joy and their deep poverty abounded unto the riches of their liberality. For to their power, yea, and beyond their power, they were willing of themselves; praying us with much intreaty that we should receive the gift, and take upon us the fellowship of ministering to the saints. And this they did, not as we hoped, but first gave their own selves to the Lord, and unto us by the will of God" (II Cor. 8:2-5).

On every hand world evangelism is suffering today from a lack of material support. Many millions of people could be reached with the Gospel were it not that Christians are so entangled in a net of covetous materialism. One is tempted to believe that nothing less than a mighty catastrophe will ever bring the church in America to the place where she will count her life not dear unto herself. However, God's preferred method of bringing His people to the position of sacrificial liberality is not one of catastrophe but the infilling of the Holy Spirit. Happy, indeed, is the Christian who walks in the joy of an abounding liberality.

With a vast percentage of the world's population sin-sick unto death, it appears grossly selfish for American Christians to make deliverance from physical sickness their primary goal. If we are to pray for physical healing, why should it not be for others—for the thousands of Christians in China, Colombia, Spain, Russia, and other countries who are going through severe physical sufferings which far surpass anything we have experienced?

The Apostle Paul said he would rather speak five words in a known tongue than 10,000 words in an unknown tongue. Why should we, who live in a world in which there are millions who have yet to hear the Gospel in their own tongue, be mainly concerned about the satisfaction which may come to our hearts through a speaking-in-tongues experience? We need to ask God for grace to proclaim His name in the language we know, to people who understand that language.

In conclusion it can be said that all true Christians are: (*a*) Born of the Spirit of God—John 3:5-7. (*b*) Baptized into the body of Christ —I Cor. 12:13. (*c*) Sealed with the Holy Spirit—Eph. 1:13; 4:30. (*d*) Indwelt by the Holy Spirit —I Cor. 6:19-20. The fact that the Christian's body is indwelt by the Spirit of God leads one to the conviction that the fullness of the Spirit depends not upon how much of the Spirit we have (this is incongruous), but how much of us He has. In other words, the fullness of the Spirit depends upon how fully He is permitted to control our lives—how yielded and obedient we are to Him.

How then does one account for the present-day phenomenon of otherwise ritualistic churches moving in the direction of that which has a tendency toward emotionalism? One can in part answer this question by asking another. How is one to understand the trend during the past thirty years of nonritualistic churches toward ritualism?

Is it not possible that a position at either side of the pendulum leaves much to be desired? Is it not reasonable to assume that some have practiced the rituals and gone through the rites without the power thereof? Are they now expressing a desire for an experience that will lift them out of the letter into the power of the Gospel? Is not this an attempt on the part of many to discover that the kingdom of God is not in word but in power?

If the answer to these questions is in the affirmative then this desire to know God in a deeper way is commendable. Caution must be exercised however lest this search for God be built upon a major premise which could lead to disappointment and disillusionment. It is this author's fear that the present trend toward tongues and healing cannot provide a foundation upon which a growing superstructure of mature Christian experience can be built.

May God give us an insatiable desire to rediscover the Person and work of the Holy Spirit in the realms of holiness, courage, unity, liberality, prayerfulness, Bible study, and a witness for Christ which is accompanied by sin-convicting, life-transforming power.

PART II
WHERE IS THE GIFT OF HEALING?

9

WHY HEALING?

AN ATTRACTIVE PUBLICATION, *Trinity Magazine,* published and distributed by The Blessed Trinity Society, Van Nuys, California, has come to my desk. This quarterly is prepared primarily by and for members of the Episcopal denomination who are interested in the gifts of the Spirit (notably healing and tongues). The editor and her Episcopal associates feel "there is no contradiction between being Episcopal and being Pentecostal." *Trinity Magazine* is contributing to the lead the Episcopal church is giving to the subject of spiritual healing within the historic churches.

This magazine is only one sign of a growing interest in healing on the part of the Episcopal church in particular and the Protestant community in general. Nor is it surprising that the subject of healing is finding a place of growing significance within the bounds of the American church. The stage is well set. The signals have been called. The die is cast. Frustrations abound on the American scene. Tensions run high and nervous breakdowns are increasingly prevalent. Men's hearts are failing them for fear, while psychiatrists become psychotics trying to meet the demands placed upon them.

What a climate this provides for a healing message! What good soil this is for seeds of hope or help. But we must never forget that the soil which nurtures wheat can also nurture tares. It is not the soil but the seed with which we are particularly concerned in this study. We believe the Bible will enable us to recognize the good seed.

It is natural that the subject of healing should have a significant place in the history of the Christian church. In the first place, the Gospel record gives to us numerous accounts of Christ's healing ministry. These accounts and His direct commands indicate that His followers would walk in His footsteps with regard to meeting the physical and temporal needs of mankind. It is, however, at this very point that the church needs to be careful in its interpretation of the miracles of Christ.

If one thing above all else is evident in Christ's miracles, it is that He was not motivated only by a desire to meet the physical and material needs of mankind. Had such been His motivation, we would be hard pressed to explain why He did not spend all or, at least, more of His time reaching the many more thousands of sick, suffering, and poverty-stricken throughout the Roman Empire.

Jesus lived in an age in which significant medical aid was lacking. The need for and opportunities to heal were legion. However, neither He nor His disciples made healing their basic ministry. When they did heal, it was fundamentally a means to an end. This is clearly seen in our Lord's careful follow-up of healing cases. A study of His dealings with those He healed reveals a consistent effort to lead them to place faith in Him as the Son of God.

No doubt there were thousands of halt, lame, blind, and sick who lived within the proximity of our Lord's ministry but who were never healed. These facts should give us cause to think twice with regard to any claim that it is the church's basic responsibility to be involved in a healing ministry.

Why did He rebuke those who sought after signs and those who followed Him only because of the bread which He could give them?

Beyond question, the fundamental motivation for Christ's healing ministry is expressed in His words, "But that ye· may know that the Son of man hath power on earth to forgive sins (he saith to the sick of the palsy,) I say unto thee, Arise, and take up thy bed, and go thy way into thine house" (Mark 2:10-11). His miracle-working ministry was motivated by His desire to establish His authority as the Son of God and to demonstrate His right to forgive sins.

There has never been a time in which the church has not been surrounded by the sick and suffering. Furthermore, it is human nature to be more concerned about physical welfare than spiritual well-being. In the face of these facts the church cannot be indifferent to human afflictions. Ever since sin entered the world, mankind has made continuous attempts to devise means to rid itself of suffering. It is reasonable, therefore, for mankind to look to the church for any possible healing which may come from that direction.

The history of healing within Christianity has

risen and fallen with periodic regularity from the time of Christ to the present day. The records reveal the story of healing movements beginning as early as A.D. 150.

It has, however, been left to the nineteenth and twentieth centuries to produce the largest rash of healing movements. Almost every contemporary religious system has some form of "divine healing" entwined within its make-up. Mormonism, Spiritism, New Thought, and Unity are some of the lesser lights in this category. Christian Science and Pentecostalism are larger and better known healing movements.

These healing programs are not limited to the Protestant branch of Christianity. Romanism has consistently fostered miracle and healing movements. Roman Catholic history is replete with the miracles performed by her saints. Her healing shrines of the present day are world-famous and are annually visited by millions of patrons. We will look into this a little farther on. But right now, what about the gift of healing?

10

WHAT IS THE "GIFT OF HEALING"?

BEFORE ONE BEGINS a search for something, it is reasonable to determine what one is looking for. This makes it necessary to ascertain what the "gift of healing" is before we attempt to answer the question of where it is.

The term "gift of healing" is never used in the Scriptures. It is always "gifts" (plural) never "gift" (singular). The fact that the plural is used suggests that each separate healing is a separate gift. The healing of the man born lame from his mother's womb (Acts 3) and the healing of Aeneas, who had been bedridden with palsy for eight years (Acts 9), are two separate "gifts" of healing, given to and exercised by Peter.

Though we cannot be dogmatic about this suggestion, it appears probable in light of the fact that the healings recorded in Acts are spasmodic rather than continual. No one who had the "gifts of healing" in Acts ever indicated that he felt called to a healing ministry. This implies that the apostles might have enjoyed the exercise of the "gifts of healing" one day and not the next. If this was the case, then each act of healing was initiated by God. It would be difficult to fit the claims of the present day "healer" into this pattern.

In order to make sure we get our subject in

proper perspective we must distinguish between the terms "divine healing," "praying for the sick," and the "gifts of healing."

The term "divine healing" does not appear in the Scriptures. There is, of course, a sense in which all healing is supernatural. Medical science performs operations and prescribes medicines, but the healing processes are ordained of God. These processes follow prescribed patterns which are established by the omniscient mind of God. However, this is not the connotation back of the term when it is used by "divine healers." They refer to a process which runs counter to natural healing laws and which falls into the realm of miracles.

Though the words "praying for the sick" are not used in the Scriptures, we are expressly taught that "the prayer of faith shall save the sick" (James 5:13-20). In this passage it is made clear that a sick brother has the privilege of calling the elders of the church to himself and asking for their prayers. Believers are exhorted to confess their faults one to another and to pray for one another that they might be healed. This type of healing ministry has probably taken place on numerous occasions throughout every age of church history.

It is noteworthy, however, that this has nothing to do with the "gifts of healing" or with most of the healing practices carried on by professional healers. Unfortunately a great deal of confusion arises from using synonymously the three terms we have just mentioned. The fact is, they are not synonymous.

As for the term "gifts of healing," it appears only three times in the New Testament. All three appearances are found in I Corinthians 12: 9, 28, 30. The term never appears again in any book of the New Testament.

It is not without import that Peter and John never refer to the subject in their epistles. Paul completely omits it in his long letter to the Romans. He never mentions it in his second letter to the Corinthians. In the rest of his wonderful prison epistles he doesn't so much as allude to the "gifts of healing." He gives no instruction in his pastoral letters on the subject. And whoever may have written the letter to the Hebrews failed to bring up the matter of healing.

The very silence of these God-inspired writings relative to the subject of the "gifts of healing" should warn us of the danger of making much of that of which God makes little.

Though we give much thought to our physical well-being in the church today, we do not get our license for doing so in the epistles. Preeminent in our prayer requests is the physical health of this friend or that. How obviously this contrasts with the recorded prayers of the Apostle Paul. To him, spiritual health, growth, and maturity were so much more significant that he hardly had time to mention physical needs in prayer.

Follow carefully the prayers offered in your next midweek prayer meeting and then contrast them with the following prayer: "For this cause I bow my knees unto the Father of our Lord

Jesus Christ, of whom the whole family in heaven and earth is named, that he would grant you, according to the riches of his glory, to be strengthened with might by his Spirit in the inner man; that Christ may dwell in your hearts by faith; that ye, being rooted and grounded in love, may be able to comprehend with all saints what is the breadth, and length, and depth, and height; and to know the love of Christ, which passeth knowledge, that ye might be filled with all the fulness of God. Now unto him that is able to do exceeding abundantly above all that we ask or think, according to the power that worketh in us, unto him be glory in the church by Christ Jesus throughout all ages, world without end. Amen" (Eph. 3:14-21).

Let us be careful, then, to keep first things first and to major in the majors. Let us also be alert to the confusion that arises out of the fact that "healers" consistently interchange such nonsynonymous terms as "divine healing," "praying for the sick," and the "gifts of healing."

The "gifts of healing" referred to in I Corinthians 12 are mentioned as one of the nine Spirit-given gifts. As is true of the other eight, this gift is imparted by the sovereign will of God to whomsoever He desires. The Scripture wording for this impartation is "dividing to every man severally as he will" (v. 11), "as it hath pleased him" (v. 18) and "according to his own will" (Heb. 2:4). Though it is perfectly in order for the child of God to "covet earnestly the best gifts" (I Cor. 12:31), yet the actual distribution of those gifts is a prerogative which belongs to

God alone.

What then is the "gifts of healing"? It requires God-given authority to say to the dead, "Arise," to the blind, "See," and to the lame, "Walk," and so on. Immediate, complete, and obvious healing follows the command. Anything less than this is something other than the "gifts of healing."

11

PETER AND THE GIFTS OF HEALING

IN THE BOOK OF ACTS (3:1-11) we are introduced to the first account of healing in the early church. Peter was the man who exercised the "gifts of healing." The man in whose life the miracle took place had a congenital deformity which affected his feet and anklebones. He was a hopeless cripple, whose lameness had been evident for forty years. His condition was a matter of public record.

"Now Peter and John went up together into the temple at the hour of prayer, being the ninth hour. And a certain man lame from his mother's womb was carried, whom they laid daily at the gate of the temple which is called Beautiful, to ask alms of them that entered into the temple; who seeing Peter and John about to go into the temple asked an alms. And Peter, fastening his eyes upon him with John, said, Look on us. And he gave heed unto them, expecting to receive something of them. Then Peter said, Silver and gold have I none; but such as I have give I thee: In the name of Jesus Christ of Nazareth rise up and walk. And he took him by the right hand, and lifted him up: and immediately his feet and ankle bones received strength. And he leaping up stood, and walked, and entered with them into the temple, walking, and leaping, and praising God. And all the people saw him walking and praising God: and they knew that it was he which sat for alms at the Beautiful gate of the temple: and they were filled with wonder and amazement at that which had happened unto him. And as the lame man which was healed held Peter and John, all the people ran together unto them in the porch that is called Solomon's, greatly wondering" (Acts 3:1-11).

There is nothing in this account which approximates our twentieth-century healing campaigns. The lame man had not responded to the advertising campaign of a "professional healer." He was not seeking for healing nor did he expect it. He was not a follower of Christ, nor did his faith or lack of it have anything to do with his healing. Furthermore, he was instantaneously and completely healed. There was no waiting, nor a suggestion that "he is being healed, but the Lord must be given time to complete it."

This immediate and complete miracle was immediately and completely obvious to those who knew and saw the man. "They knew it was he." No research was necessary to establish the validity of the case.

Peter at once disclaimed any credit for the healing. He was deeply disturbed that people should think it could be credited to his personal power or holiness. He said, "And his name, through faith in his name, has made this man strong whom ye see and know: yea, the faith which is by him hath given him this perfect soundness in the presence of you all" (Acts 3:16).

We turn now to the next account of Peter's

relation to the subject of healing. In Acts 5:14-16 we read, "And believers were the more added to the Lord, multitudes both of men and women. Insomuch that they brought forth the sick into the streets, and laid them on beds and couches, that at the least the shadow of Peter passing by might overshadow some of them. There came also a multitude out of the cities round about unto Jerusalem, bringing sick folks, and them which were vexed with unclean spirits: and they were healed every one."

This is the only "healing campaign" in which Peter was ever involved. Nor was it set up for him by an advance agent. It was spontaneous and unplanned. It did not involve the taking of medical histories or the signing of cards on the part of those to be healed. There were no rituals nor techniques which had to be followed. Furthermore, nothing was done in secret.

All of these facts contrast sharply with twentieth-century campaigns. But the most startling contrast is found in the statement, ". . . and they were healed *every one*" (italics mine). This statement places the true "gifts of healing" into a category completely apart from that which is claimed today. Those who experience *provable healings* of congenital or obvious deformities represent a very small minority of those who claim healing in present-day campaigns. It is in fact questionable whether they can be found at all. Another point of contrast: Peter did not demand faith on the part of those desiring to be healed.

It is not without significance that we have no

further record of Peter ever taking part in a "healing campaign." He was no "professional" in this. As a true man of God he was used by God when and as God directed. His main job was soul-winning, and to this he held. Like the rest of the apostles, Peter felt it more important to give himself to prayer and the ministry of the Word (Acts 6:4). This is hardly characteristic of those who are in the divine healing "business" today.

Acts 9:32-43 gives us the last two recorded miracles in which Peter was involved. The first case had to do with a man named Aeneas, "which had kept his bed eight years and was sick of the palsy."

As in the healing of the man born lame, so in the case of Aeneas, his healing was instantaneous, unostentatious, and complete. The miracle was obvious to all and resulted in many turning to the Lord. Though there must have been many others in Lydda who needed healing, Peter was led to exercise the "gifts of healing" only upon this one man.

We are then given the account of the raising of Dorcas from the dead. "Then Peter arose and went with them. When he was come, they brought him into the upper chamber: and all the widows stood by him weeping, and shewing the coats and garments which Dorcas made, while she was with them. But Peter put them all forth, and kneeled down, and prayed; and turning him to the body said, Tabitha, arise. And she opened her eyes: and when she saw Peter, she sat up. And he gave her his hand, and lifted her up, and when he had called the saints and widows, presented her alive. And it was known throughout all Joppa; and many believed in the Lord" (Acts 9:39-42).

Perhaps the most impressive aspect of this miracle was the unimpressive way in which it was performed. No advertising or elaborate preparations preceded the miracle nor did any propaganda follow it. One could not overestimate the amount of fanfare which would accompany such an affair today should our "divine healers" be able to raise the dead.

And right here we are brought face to face with some devastating questions. If a man truly has the "gifts of healing," is there any reason why he should fall short of the power to raise the dead? Is there any basic difference between the power that gives new life to crippled limbs and paralyzed muscles and the power that raises the dead? Should not the power to raise the dead be the criterion upon which a man's professed "gifts of healing" are evaluated? Peter and Paul both exercised the gifts of healing and both raised the dead.

We face one final thought in respect to Peter's exercise of the gifts of healing. There is no conclusive evidence that Peter ever used it in regard to a sick *believer*. If Dorcas was a believer before her resurrection, at least she had nothing to say about the miracle which took place in her life. This stands in bold contrast to those who insist that the effectiveness of the gifts of healing is altered by the faith of those who desire to be healed. We shall see this fact more clearly as we consider others in the Book of Acts who were healed.

In summary it can be claimed that healing held a comparatively incidental place in Peter's ministry. Nor did he refer to his healing experiences or to the "gifts of healing" in his epistles. One is therefore left with the impression that if Peter were preaching and writing today, his theme would not be healing.

On the other hand Peter gave a great deal of space in his epistles to the subject of suffering. The following phrases suggest the theme of his first epistle: "heaviness through manifold temptations," "the trial of your faith," "endure grief, suffering wrongfully," "that ye suffer for well doing," "if ye suffer for righteousness' sake," "the fiery trial which is to try you," "as ye are partakers of Christ's sufferings," and "wherefore let them that suffer *according to the will of God* [italics mine] commit the keeping of their souls to him in well doing, as unto a faithful Creator."

Of course, one could argue that Peter was fortifying scattered believers with regard to suffering which results from persecution. And the context of I Peter reveals that this is a perfectly correct deduction. However, we are led to ask, What, after all, is the basic difference between suffering from arthritis, blindness, or typhoid fever and suffering from hunger, or from a sword wound as a result of persecution?

As we shall see in a later chapter, suffering does play a significant part in the dealings of God with His children. Nor does God give believers any blanket promise of deliverance from suffering. If anyone gives us clear teaching on this subject, it is Peter, who, on rare occasions, under the sovereign control and timing of God, exercised the gifts of healing. Strange, isn't it, that he did not suggest that the needs of his suffering readers would be met by miracles or by the gifts of healing? Or did Peter realize that there is something gloriously important about suffering "according to the will of God"?

12

PHILIP AND THE GIFTS OF HEALING

APART FROM THOSE performed by Peter and Paul,
only in Philip's ministry does Acts record miracles
of healing. Barnabas, Silas, Timothy, James and
Acts. Barnabas, Silas, Timothy, James, and
Apollos are only a few of those who carried on
effective ministries for God who apparently did
not perform miracles or have the gifts of
healing.

The account of Philip's experience is given to
us in Acts 8:5-8: "Then Philip went down to
the city of Samaria, and preached Christ unto
them. And the people with one accord gave
heed unto those things which Philip spake, hearing and seeing the miracles which he did. For
unclean spirits, crying with loud voice, came out
of many that were possessed with them: and
many taken with palsies, and that were lame,
were healed. And there was great joy in that
city."

We are first introduced to Philip in Acts 6:5,
where we meet him as one of the seven men
appointed by the early church to take care of
"serving tables." Philip was not an apostle or a
full-time preacher. He was a godly layman. The
fact, therefore, that he had the gifts of healing
would indicate that God was pleased to give this
gift to others than "professional" preachers.

Samaria provided the setting for the miracles

and healings wrought through Philip. Unclean spirits were cast out, the paralyzed and the lame were healed, and many believed. The healings were not performed among or for believers. However, it appears that the Samaritans' willingness to give heed to Philip's preaching grew out of the fact that they saw the miracles which he did. In giving heed to his message they became believers. This is implied in the statement, "There was great joy in that city."

Though Philip became an evangelist (Acts 21:8), and though he must have had years of effective ministry, there is no other record of miracles ever accompanying that ministry. He never became a "healer."

Evidently the manifestation of healing power in Philip's ministry at Samaria was for the direct purpose of establishing the authority of the Gospel message and the church among the Samaritans.

13

PAUL AND THE GIFTS OF HEALING

IT IS IN THE RECORD of the ministry of Paul that the gift of healing is mentioned most frequently. He possessed this gift and made use of it several occasions. However, the times when he did not make use of the gifts of healing are probably more significant than the times when he did.

Paul's first recorded use of the gift is in Acts 14. The account reads, "And there sat a certain man at Lystra, impotent in his feet, being a cripple from his mother's womb, who never had walked: the same heard Paul speak: who steadfastly beholding him, and perceiving that he had faith to be healed, said with a loud voice, Stand upright on thy feet. And he leaped and walked."

As was true of the lame man whose healing is recorded in the third chapter of Acts, this man at Lystra had a congenital deformity which was obvious to all. This cripple listened intently while Paul preached the Gospel. It is possible that, in his preaching, Paul had referred to some of the miracles performed by Christ. At any rate, there was born in the heart of this cripple a faith in the fact that he could be healed. Paul perceived this and, turning to the lame man, said with a loud voice, "Stand upright on thy feet." The healing was instantaneous and complete. This is characteristic of every healing recorded in the Book of Acts.

There are two significant lessons which can be learned from this particular case. In the first place, this is the only account in the Book of Acts in which the faith of the one healed is mentioned. The fact that "he had faith to be healed" does not necessarily imply that he was a follower of Christ. It could, of course, be assumed that as a result of the miracle he became a follower of Christ.

In the second place, the results of this miracle leave for us a significant warning. I refer to the tendency of human nature to worship the one through whom the miracle is wrought rather than to worship the One who is the source of the miracle. Paul and Barnabas could scarcely restrain the people from offering sacrifices unto them. Unfortunately some present-day "healers" have apparently found it impossible to restrain themselves from accepting the praise, adulation, and sacrifices which people give them. Some even appear to seek it.

We turn now to Acts 16 to find Paul's next exercise of the gifts of healing. In verses sixteen to eighteen we read, "And it came to pass, as we went to prayer, a certain damsel possessed with a spirit of divination met us, which brought her masters much gain by soothsaying: the same followed Paul and us, and cried, saying, These men are the servants of the most high God, which shew unto us the way of salvation. And this did she many days, but Paul, being grieved, turned and said to the spirit, I command thee in the name of Jesus Christ to come out of her. And he came out the same hour."

The following facts are noteworthy in these verses: First, there is a "spirit of divination" which can and does possess human bodies. This spirit is an evil spirit and is used for evil ends. This spirit, as all evil spirits, recognizes the servants of the Most High God. He is also aware of the "way of salvation." Second, Paul spoke directly to the spirit. He addressed the spirit in the name of Jesus Christ, commanding him to leave the damsel. The spirit obeyed and the damsel was healed.

One wonders how many evil-spirit-possessed men and women there are both in and out of our institutions today, who could be healed if there were those who had authority in the name of Christ to cast out these spirits.

We turn to Acts 19 to find the first of two accounts in which the Apostle Paul took part in a mass healing program. The experience is described in these words: "And God wrought special miracles by the hands of Paul; so that from his body were brought unto the sick handkerchiefs or aprons, and the diseases departed from them, and the evil spirits went out of them" (vv. 11-12).

It is not the similarity between this recorded experience of Paul and the modern mass healing movements but rather the contrast, which is obvious. Paul was not holding a healing campaign. There were no prolonged preliminaries in which preaching and praise services were used in a calculated attempt to work his audience into an emotional pitch. There is no record of any hand-raising, arm-waving, repetition of the name of Jesus, or shouting. No questions were asked about faith, and no books were written about the experience.

Though the Apostle Paul was in many other cities in which there were hundreds of sick and demon-possessed, we have no other account of handkerchiefs or aprons ever being distributed among the sick in those cities. This was apparently a once-for-all experience which never took place again.

In Acts 20:7-12, Paul becomes an instrument in the hand of God to raise up Eutychus. The account informs us that Paul embraced the corpse but, apparently, did not speak to it. He simply informed those who were standing around, "His life is in him." Paul then continued to preach until daylight, and the next day he "sailed unto Assos." We wonder how much publicity would be sought today should some "healer" perform such a miracle.

Paul's last recorded healing ministry is in Acts 28, where we are told the "father of Publius lay sick of a fever and of a bloody flux: to whom Paul entered in, and prayed, and laid his hands on him, and healed him." This resulted in "others also which had diseases in the island" coming and being healed.

It is questionable that any of Paul's healings involved believers. We are, in fact, impressed with the fact that specific mention is made of believers who were not healed. Paul left sick Trophimus at Miletus (II Tim. 4:20). He refers to Epaphroditus as being nigh unto death for the work of Christ (Phil. 2:27). He exhorts Timothy to take a little wine for his illness (I Tim. 5:23). He refers to the believers at Corinth, who came behind in no gift (I Cor. 1:7); yet Paul tells them, "Many are weak and sickly among you, and many sleep" (I Cor. 11:30). Paul himself had a "thorn in the flesh," which was probably a physical affliction.

How far removed is all of this from the claims, teachings, and practices of present-day healers. The simple fact is, healing campaigns would not have to be advertised if they were genuine. Neither Peter, Philip, nor Paul ever capitalized on the divine healing issue. They did not promote themselves as healers.

As suggested in the opening paragraph of this chapter, there is real significance in the fact that Paul preached in many towns and cities in which he did not exercise the gifts of healing. Nor is it without significance that he never urged his fellow workers, Barnabas, Silas, Luke, Mark, Timothy, to seek this gift. It is certainly obvious that Paul was not a healing campaigner.

There are also some lessons to learn from the fact that Paul does not mention the subject of the gifts of healing in any of his other epistles. The sixteen chapters of Romans, the thirteen chapters of Second Corinthians, the six chapters of Galatians, the six chapters of Ephesians, to mention several of Paul's books, contain no reference to the subject. This argument from silence is not without import. He is not silent about spiritual health and maturity, about

Christian conduct and the great doctrinal themes in any of his epistles. Why should he then be so silent about the gifts of healing?

Contrast Paul's silence on this subject with the writings of the "healers" of today. Their magazines are filled with little of anything other than healing. Sermons, polemics, studies, and testimonies are all geared to the subject of healing to the point where the reader is left with the feeling that his physical well-being must be the most important thing in life. This is not the impression Paul leaves with his readers.

We must conclude, therefore, that in the life and ministry of the Apostle Paul the "gifts of healing" were sovereignly imparted to him on comparatively infrequent occasions. They were apparently used to establish the authority of Paul's preaching among the Gentiles in particular. They were never used as an audience-gaining or offering-getting gimmick. They were incidental to his Gospel preaching—nor did he feel called to a healing ministry.

14

THESE ARE NOT
THE GIFTS OF HEALING

WHATEVER ELSE is added to one's knowledge from the following accounts of healing, one thing is certain. They are not the "gifts of healing." They do not fit into the pattern of First Corinthians. Let us look at a few of these records.

The Rev. R. J. Womble of Christ Episcopal Church, Little Rock, Arkansas, says: "One way to receive the power and presence of the healing Christ is to take of the holy communion . . . Receive His divine and healing love in the consecrated bread and wine.

". . . because of God's will for man's wholeness in this life, and because of man's need for mental and physical health, *the healing ministry of Jesus is being rediscovered* [italics mine] and is now in the process of steady and widespread growth. Christ's healing ministry in the Episcopal Church is coming in a very calm, sane, dignified, and effective way. The Episcopal Church is giving leadership to hundreds of churches of other denominations.

"Dr. Alfred Price, Rector of St. Stephen's Church in Philadelphia, keeps a record of what happens to the people who come under his healing ministry. At his last report, 40 percent of the people he and his prayer group prayed for were made well."

To Rev. Womble's claim that this represents a

rediscovery of "the healing ministry of Jesus," we would simply ask, In what way? Are the similarities between the healing ministry of Christ and the present-day program as evident as the contrasts?

In her book, *A Reporter Finds God Through Spiritual Healing,* Emily Gardner Neal records numerous healings. We will look at just one of them.

"Case #94 . . . E. R., age 21. Diagnosis: paralysis of entire left side due to pressure on the brain caused by birth injury. Condition inoperable. Patient was completely cured through spiritual healing. Hers was a gradual healing, occurring over a period of three years."

Though there may be some relationship between this "spiritual healing" and the teachings of James 5 concerning praying for the sick, there certainly isn't the slightest connection with the "gifts of healing." It appears that most of the healings taking place in this "spiritual healing" movement require special prayer efforts often accompanied with the laying on of hands. The time element also seems significant. A period of days, months, or even years may elapse before complete restoration of health is experienced.

No religious group has been more consistent in its claims of healing than the adherents of Christian Science. The following professed case of healing illustrates these claims:

"About five years ago I suffered from what I thought was an abscessed tooth. I did prayerful, metaphysical work as we are taught to do in Science, but the condition became worse. There was swelling and pain, and after a week, during which I lost much weight, I could not move my jaws. Friends who were not interested in Christian Science expressed great concern about my condition, and a dentist's son who was one of them said that in his opinion I had lockjaw. At this point I decided unwisely to see a dentist if only to find out what was wrong.

"The next day after the dentist had examined the X-ray pictures he said there was nothing wrong with my tooth but he recommended that I go to a hospital for attention immediately. He said he believed I had lockjaw and a strangulation of some sort. After I had left him I realized I had to free myself from the mesmerism of mortal mind to which I had succumbed.

"I drove to the office of a Christian Science practitioner. After I had told her all, she asked me whether I preferred to go to a hospital or to work the problem out with God. Of course, I chose God. I had no fear, for I knew that if we put our trust in God, He will keep us. That was on a Monday night.

"On Tuesday I called the practitioner. She assured me of man's oneness with God as the expression of His being. That night I knew that my healing was at hand. I read many helpful statements from *Science and Health* by Mrs. Eddy. I went to sleep after midnight and awoke in the morning free from all pain. I felt like a new man, and on the fourth day I enjoyed a hearty meal. I missed only five days away from my work" (*Christian Science Sentinel*, August, 1962, p. 1491).

Regardless of how one may explain this man's

experience, it is apparent that it does not have the remotest relation to the "gifts of healing." It is this writer's personal conviction that psychosomatic recoveries from imagined illness, actual miracles performed by the "father of lies" for the purpose of deception, or the natural healing processes of nature can explain the healings which are claimed by such organizations as Christian Science and Roman Catholicism.

The crass commercialism, the open idolatry, and the not infrequent immorality which are so often found at Catholic healing shrines such as Lourdes all bear testimony to the fact that whatever healing is professed has not followed any Scriptural pattern. Whatever these healings are, they are unrelated to the "gifts of healing."

How about the "professional" healing program within the Protestant world? Is this the place in which we will find the "gifts of healing"? Perhaps a little investigation will answer these questions.

"You are to have a healing ministry as long as you live." This statement quoted from one of America's most prominent healers seems to place him in a unique position. It sets a precedent. To my knowledge there is no one in Scripture who was specifically set apart for a healing ministry or to whom God gave assurance that he would carry on such a ministry as long as he lived.

Though this gentleman claims to be the recipient of a God-given healing ministry, he is ever so careful to emphasize the great importance of faith on the part of those who seek healing. This immediately puts his ministry in a category other than the one in which the healing ministries of Peter, Paul, and Philip are found. The following testimony illustrates the point:

"I went through the prayer line, but I didn't feel I was completely healed. I had pain again and I was afraid to step out in faith and claim my healing . . . In 1953 my husband took me to another . . . Crusade in Amarillo, Texas. *I was determined to have faith* and to receive complete healing. [Italics mine.] I was prayed for again. By the next morning I knew everything was all right. I felt so peaceful, so wonderful."

The evangelist through whom this woman received her healing said to those who were in the "invalid room," "You can receive your healing tonight, *if you will believe and exercise your faith.*" (Italics mine.)

It would be difficult to fit the experience of this woman or the statements of the healer into the Book of Acts or I Corinthians 12.

It is this writer's opinion that the "gifts of healing" are not found within the circle of "divine healers" today. Both the techniques and results of today's professional healing ministries stand in such bold contrast to what is recorded in the Book of Acts, that one fails to see any similarity or connection between the two. By this I am simply saying that if there has been anyone during the thirty years of my observation who has exercised the true "gifts of healing," I have never met or read of that person.

How then does one account for either the actual or apparent healings which take place in healing campaigns?

Before answering the question let us make careful note of the following facts: (1) There are extremely few if any demonstratable healings which have involved those with congenital deformities obvious to the public. (2) A great percentage of those who have sought healing at the hands of "divine healers" have never received healing regardless of the form of illness or affliction they had.

Having recognized these facts, we still must face up to the question as to how healings which have occurred or do occur take place.

The answer is fourfold. In the first place, it is acknowledged by medical science that a great percentage of sickness is a form of hypochondria. The encyclopedia describes this as "a morbid condition characterized by an increase in sensitivity to changes in the internal organs, by stimulation of the symptoms of any of several diseases, and in its advanced stages by anxiety and melancholia."

The hypochondriac often suffers from some disease for which no actual functional or structural disorder can be discovered. His illness is psychosomatically induced. A loss of appetite, irritability, sleeplessness are three of several effects which may follow in the train of such a mental attitude. This is a case of mind over matter. Some doctors estimate that as high as 70 percent of those who are ill in America either just think they are ill or have thought themselves into illness.

Illness which can be psychosomatically induced can often be psychosomatically destroyed.

Knowing this, the psychiatrist does his best to influence the hypochondriac into a change of thought pattern. The growing need for and number of psychologists and psychiatrists is irrefutable evidence that a great deal of sickness today involves the metaphysical.

It was probably Mary Baker Eddy's realization of this which led to the establishment of Christian Science. The astounding growth of Christian Science and the "healings" within it add their testimony to the reality of psychosomatically induced illnesses and healings. Unity, New Thought, Theosophy, Couéism, Dowieism, and Yogism are but a few of the movements which have followed in the tide of "divine healing" and have capitalized on the theory of mind over matter.

This is not to suggest that psychological healings are either dangerous or wrong. Many splendid things have been accomplished in the restoration of health to the ill as a result of psychiatric counseling, on the part of Christian psychiatrists and pastors as well as unbelieving psychiatrists. The danger lies in the fact that men make a religion of "mind over matter," and attribute miracles to God which are not miracles at all. Then for the sake of gain or fame they establish a religious cult which is contrary to the work of Him whom they profess to glorify.

Psychosomatically induced healings cannot honestly be related to the "gifts of healing."

In the second place, healings have been and can be wrought by the powers of darkness. The enemy of the souls of men is a miracle worker. He can both bring affliction and destruction upon individuals or groups. The afflictions and deaths which he brought into Job's home illustrate this fact. Satan can perform miracles for the apparent good of his followers. The miracles wrought by the hands of Egypt's magicians demonstrate this.

Jesus warned His disciples that false prophets would arise who would work miracles and signs sufficient to lead the elect astray if it were possible. Paul tells us in Second Thessalonians that the working of Satan is "with all power and signs and lying wonders, and with all deceivableness of unrighteousness." In the Book of the Revelation we find the False Prophet and Beast performing miracles calculated to deceive and destroy many.

We cannot, therefore, cast aside the fact that Satan can be a source of healing. But this obviously has no relation to the "gifts of healing."

A third source of healing is medical science. Our hospitals bear testimony to the importance of this source. Happy is that people who are blessed with hospitals. Nor is it without significance that the Christian message has always been the forerunner of medical advance on the mission fields of the world. No one can question the value of the contribution medical science has made to the physical health and welfare of millions of people.

This ministry, however, does not fit within the category of "gifts of healing" and, hence, further consideration of it is not needful.

The fourth source of healing is God. In this regard we refer to His bestowal of the "gifts of healing" upon individuals. We have seen these "gifts of healing" demonstrated in the Book of Acts. I can find no convincing evidence that they are being demonstrated today. If there is any individual today who has under God the authority to say to the dead, "Arise," to the blind, "See," to the deaf, "Hear," to the lame, "Walk," then I have not met him or read of him. The "healings" which do take place at the hands of "divine healers" today must, therefore, come from one of the first three sources which we have just considered, totally apart from the "gifts of healing."

That God does graciously restore the sick to health in answer to the prayers of His people, when it pleases Him, the author has no doubt. But this fits into James 5 and not I Corinthians 12.

15

HEALING AND THE CURSE OF SIN

THERE ARE THOSE who confuse the issue of healing by claiming that because the Christian is "in Christ" the curse of sin has been removed from him. He has, therefore, no right to remain in a position subject to the effects of sin. Sickness is to be rebuked and rejected in the name of Christ, and healing is to be expected at all times. The probable exceptions would be admitted only in cases of unbelief or unconfessed sin.

But let's take a look at an individual who has faith and in whose life there is no unconfessed sin. According to the theory just suggested, it would be accurate to assume that he would always be healed and that sickness or illness could not long abide in his body.

Here is Mr. Amundsen. He is a holy man of God. He has no doubts as to the willingness and power of God to heal. Although he has always enjoyed good health, he is now seventy years old, and a physical checkup reveals several complications. Arthritis has begun to take its toll in his ankles and the knuckles of his hands. His teeth have begun to decay, and this has led to an infection in the lower jaw which will necessitate the removal of all his lower teeth. His eyesight is poor and growing worse every year. He will have to have glasses if he is going to be able to read. A hearing aid will also be necessary if he wants to continue hearing the Sunday morning services.

Looking at Mr. Amundsen objectively, what are we going to do about him? If we believe it is never the will of God for a Christian to be sick, we will pray for his healing—not just in part but completely. We will expect God to heal him of his arthritis, jaw infection, poor eyesight, and deafness. However, this is not what is generally done. And here is where a glaring inconsistency shows up. We are quite ready to pray for the healing of someone who is suffering from cancer or typhoid fever, and so forth. A few might even go so far as to ask God to heal broken bones apart from the use of medical science. But where are those who are so convinced that ill health is never in the plan of God that they will pray for those who are suffering as a result of that normal degeneration or breakdown of the body which accompanies old age?

Poor sight in old age is an affliction from which many an aged saint would like to be delivered. But somehow those who pray for the sick seem prepared to pray for a child whose eyesight needs correction, while placing the crippling accompaniments of old age in a category concerning which prayer for healing has no room. The inconsistency of this is self-evident.

It would, of course, be nice if every sickness, including the inevitable signs of old age, could be eradicated through divine healing. However, the question arises as to just when the human body begins to lose its natural forces. At what age in life is it at the apex of its health and

91

strength? When this is answered (and it would vary with each individual), then any indication of a lessening of those natural forces would present a call for healing. If healing took place, the individual concerned could live on an "eternal youth" basis, assuming that each time an infirmity appeared he would simply receive divine healing.

As fantastic as this sounds, it represents the honest and logical conclusion to which one is led when he insists that it is never the will of God for a child of God to be ill and, hence, it is always the will of God to heal.

We now come to the subject of the curse of sin and its relationship to the health of the Christian. In Genesis 3:16-19 we read: "Unto the woman he said, I will greatly multiply thy sorrow and thy conception; in sorrow thou shalt bring forth children; and thy desire shall be to thy husband, and he shall rule over thee. And unto Adam he said, Because thou hast hearkened unto the voice of thy wife, and hast eaten of the tree, of which I commanded thee, saying, Thou shalt not eat of it: cursed is the ground for thy sake; in sorrow shalt thou eat of it all the days of thy life; thorns also and thistles shall it bring forth to thee; and thou shalt eat the herb of the field; in the sweat of thy face shalt thou eat bread, till thou return unto the ground; for out of it wast thou taken: for dust thou art, and unto dust shalt thou return."

There are those who believe the Christian has been removed from the curse of sin. They argue that because the child of God is "in Christ" the curse of sin cannot touch him. Though it is true that the believer can and should enjoy a victory over sin which is unknown to the unregenerate, it is just as true that as long as we are on earth we are subject to the frailties of a sin-cursed body and a sin-cursed world.

Becoming a Christian does not deliver a woman from the pain of birth pangs. Like her non-Christian sisters she brings forth children with suffering. Though she is comforted and fortified in her suffering by the presence of the Lord, she is not delivered from suffering.

Becoming a Christian does not deliver a man from tilling soil which is cursed with thorns and thistles or from earning his bread by the sweat of his brow. Nor does he have any right to sit back and ask God to rid his fields of thistles or to supply his needs apart from earning them by the sweat of his brow. The Scriptures are clear-cut in their teaching that the man who will not work does not deserve to eat. He who provides not (by the sweat of his brow) for his family is worse than an infidel, for he has denied the faith.

There is no basis for believing that when a person becomes a Christian his body, which was born under the curse of sin, is suddenly transformed into a body which is no longer subject to that curse or to the temptations which come from a sin-cursed world. A new desire to take proper care of one's body motivated by a new understanding of the fact that it has become the temple of the Holy Spirit could certainly slow down the general deterioration which accompanies age. But this could also take place in the body of a non-Christian who for some other reason felt that clean, disciplined living was advantageous.

If the Christian through new birth is delivered from the moral weakness to which the human body is subject, then there is no meaning to numerous negative warnings in the Bible. Why do the Scriptures command the Christian not to be given to wine, not to be greedy of filthy lucre, not to be double-tongued, and not to be covetous, if he is not subject to these things? Why is the believer warned against lust and fornication apart from the fact that his body can become an instrument of these things?

What significance is there in the following two verses if the believer's body is not subject to sin? "Wherefore let him that thinketh he standeth take heed lest he fall. There hath no temptation taken you but such as is common to man: but God is faithful, who will not suffer you to be tempted above that ye are able; but will with the temptation also make a way to escape, that ye may be able to bear it" (I Cor. 10:12-13).

No, it is not true that the believer can claim health on the grounds that his body has been delivered from the curse of sin which has been passed on to him from the first Adam. Not until he has received a glorified body from the Last Adam will this be true. The fact that death claims the Christian as well as the non-Christian is irrefutable proof that the body of the believer has not been delivered from the curse of sin. But, blessed be God, he has been delivered from the condemnation of it.

Our position "in Christ" cannot, then, form a

premise upon which we can insist upon healing. It is, however, the position from which all our petitions are made to God.

16

THE CHRISTIAN'S CLAIM TO HEALTH

THE OLD TESTAMENT records many promises made by God to Israel concerning physical and material prosperity. The Pentateuch contains many of them, and several of the historical and prophetical books reiterate them. Perhaps Deuteronomy 28 is the classic chapter on the subject. The first fourteen verses of this chapter enumerate the blessings which God promised to bestow upon Israel if she would observe and do all His commandments.

"Blessed shalt thou be in the city, and blessed shalt thou be in the field. Blessed shall be the fruit of thy body, and the fruit of thy ground, and the fruit of thy cattle, the increase of thy kine, and the flocks of thy sheep. Blessed shall be thy basket and thy store. Blessed shalt thou be when thou comest in, and blessed shalt thou be when thou goest out.

"The Lord shall cause thine enemies that rise up against thee to be smitten before thy face: they shall come out against thee one way, and flee before thee seven ways. The Lord shall command the blessing upon thee in thy storehouses, and in all that thou settest thine hand unto; and he shall bless thee in the land which the Lord thy God giveth thee.

"The Lord shall establish thee an holy people unto himself, as he hath sworn unto thee, if thou shalt keep the commandments of the Lord thy God, and walk in his ways. And all people of the earth shall see that thou art called by the name of the Lord; and they shall be afraid of thee. And the Lord shall make thee plenteous in goods, in the fruit of thy body, and in the fruit of thy cattle, and in the fruit of thy ground, in the land which the Lord sware unto thy fathers to give thee. The Lord shall open unto thee his good treasure, the heaven to give the rain unto thy land in his season, and to bless all the work of thine hand: and thou shalt lend unto many nations, and thou shalt not borrow" (Deut. 28:3-12).

It is both obvious and noteworthy that the blessings promised were physical and material. Likewise the curses pronounced upon Israel in the remaining portion of Deuteronomy 28, if Israel did not obey the commands of the Lord God, would affect the health and wealth of the nation.

Israel was to be God's "earthly" people. This cannot be refuted. It was God's desire to set the children of Israel on high above all the nations of the earth. They were to be so blessed of God that all the people of the earth would recognize them as chosen people of God.

God's protection of and provision for His people in Egypt as well as His watch-care of the children of Israel during forty years in the wilderness illustrates this point: "And I have led you forty years in the wilderness: your clothes are not waxen old upon you, and thy shoe is not waxen old upon thy foot" (Deut. 29:5). Who ever heard of clothes and shoes lasting forty years? And who ever heard of God providing meat and manna in the wilderness for any nation except Israel?

Prosperity and protection were to be enjoyed by the children of Israel as long as they walked in the statutes of the Lord and kept His commandments. They were to dwell in safety, to chase their enemies, and to rule over them. They were to enjoy prosperity. The fruit of the womb, the fruit of the trees, the increase of the fields, and the multiplication of cattle were all to be theirs. Health and wealth were to characterize the nation of Israel.

On the other hand, poverty, plagues, and bondage were to be Israel's lot if she refused to walk with God. History bears ample testimony to the awful enslavement and suffering through which these people have passed through the centuries.

Neither the blessings nor curses pronounced upon Israel are applicable to the Christian. This is not to say that the principle, "As a man sows, so shall he reap" does not apply to the Christian. It does mean that God has not made to the Church (His *heavenly* people) the same promises nor pronounced upon them the same curses as to Israel (His *earthly* people). There is overwhelming evidence in the New Testament that the riches of God's grace so freely bestowed upon the Church are neither physical nor material. Both health and wealth were proofs of His favor upon Israel. This cannot be applied to the Christian as an individual nor to the Church as a whole. Many godly couples have been childless, many a Christian saint has lived in comparative poverty, and many a Christian family or community has been trampled under the cruel heel of an oppressing government. The early church accepted the persecution and suffering through which it passed as a part of the will of God. The early church prayed not for deliverance from opposition but for courage to face it.

Because the believer's body is a temple of the Holy Spirit and thus a vessel for God's glory, it needs to be properly cared for. It is to be an instrument unto righteousness. Its fleshly cravings are to be curbed and its appetites guarded. The Christian is warned to be temperate in the physical aspects of his life. He is to follow those principles of cleanliness, exercise, eating, and rest which contribute to good health.

On the other hand the Christian is in no position to demand immunity from sickness or suffering. If and as he lives "godly in Christ Jesus" he can expect opposition from the world, which may entail physical suffering. The life of Paul vividly demonstrates this. The Christian may also so labor for the Lord as to jeopardize his health. This is apparently what happened to Paul's fellow soldier Epaphroditus. "For he longed after you all, and was full of heaviness, because that ye had heard that he had been sick. For indeed he was sick nigh unto death: . . . Because for the work of Christ he was nigh unto death, not regarding his life, to supply your lack of service toward me" (Phil. 2:26-27,30).

The believer's citizenship is in Heaven. His

affections are set upon things which are above. He looks for a city whose builder and maker is God. He is, therefore, not given to overmuch concern with regard to his physical or material well-being. Health and wealth are of secondary importance. The believer's basic claim to health is spiritual. He is to be strong in the Lord though he may be weak of body. He is to enter into the riches of grace in Christ Jesus though he may be poor in earthly treasures. His attitude is expressed by Paul: "Neither count I my life dear unto myself, so that I might finish my course with joy" (Acts 20:24).

17

THE SANCTITY OF SUFFERING

THERE ARE THOSE who feel that for God to allow any sickness, or suffering, or trouble to come to His children is evidence that He "is either not omnipotent or not altogether good." They argue that a good father would not allow his children to suffer if he had the power to withhold suffering.

Such reasoning reveals an appalling ignorance of the Scriptures, of the nature of God, and of the true values of life. There is little meaning to any of the following verses apart from the significant place sorrow, suffering, and sickness can play in the Christian life.

"Blessed be God, even the Father of our Lord Jesus Christ, the Father of mercies, and the God of all comfort; Who comforteth us in all our tribulation, that we may be able to comfort them which are in any trouble, by the comfort wherewith we ourselves are comforted of God. For as the sufferings of Christ abound in us, so our consolation also aboundeth by Christ. And whether we be afflicted, it is for your consolation and salvation, which is effectual in the enduring of the same sufferings which we also suffer: or whether we be comforted, it is for your consolation and salvation. And our hope of you is stedfast, knowing, that as ye are partakers of the sufferings, so shall ye be also of the consolation" (II Cor. 1:3-7).

"When thou passest through the waters, I will be with thee; and through the rivers, they shall not overflow thee: when thou walkest through the fire, thou shalt not be burned; neither shall the flame kindle upon thee" (Isa. 43:2).

"Before I was afflicted I went astray: but now have I kept thy word" (Ps. 119:67).

"It is good for me that I have been afflicted; that I might learn thy statutes" (Ps. 119:71).

"And ye have forgotten the exhortation which speaketh unto you as unto children, My son, despise not thou the chastening of the Lord, nor faint when thou art rebuked of him: for whom the Lord loveth he chasteneth, and scourgeth every son whom he receiveth. If ye endure chastening, God dealeth with you as with sons; for what son is he whom the father chasteneth not? But if ye be without chastisement, whereof all are partakers, then are ye bastards, and not sons.

"Furthermore we have had fathers of our flesh which corrected us, and we gave them reverence: shall we not much rather be in subjection unto the Father of spirits, and live? For they verily for a few days chastened us after their own pleasure; but he for our profit, that we might be partakers of his holiness. Now no chastening for the present seemeth to be joyous, but grievous: nevertheless afterward it yieldeth the peaceable fruit of righteousness unto them which are exercised thereby" (Heb. 12:5-11).

"If I must needs glory, I will glory of the things which concern mine infirmities" (II Cor. 11:30).

"And lest I should be exalted above measure through the abundance of the revelations, there was given to me a thorn in the flesh, the messenger of Satan to buffet me, lest I should be exalted above measure. For this thing I besought the Lord thrice, that it might depart from me. And he said unto me, My grace is sufficient for thee: for my strength is made perfect in weakness. Most gladly therefore will I rather glory in my infirmities, that the power of Christ may rest upon me. Therefore I take pleasure in infirmities, in reproaches, in necessities, in persecutions, in distresses for Christ's sake: for when I am weak, then am I strong" (II Cor. 12:7-10).

The human soul is stunted when it is too much sheltered from the winds of adversity. There is something about sorrow and suffering which puts steel into the soul. How great were the lessons Job learned from the sufferings through which he passed. He emerged from his trials as gold tried in the fire. He saw the frailty of his own nature and the glory of God in a way in which he had not before seen them. In triumphant faith he cried, "Though he slay me, yet will I trust in him."

If there is any lesson to be learned from the Book of Job and from First Peter, it is that suffering does have a place in the will of God for the child of God. Christ suffered in the flesh, leaving us an example, that we should follow in His steps (I Peter 2:21). Trials, afflictions, and weaknesses all make a contribution toward conforming us to the image of Christ. The trial of our faith is more precious than gold (I Peter 1:7). Nor are we to be overly concerned about the fiery trial which is to try us (I Peter 4:12). It was a proper understanding of and attitude toward these things which enabled Paul to glory in his sufferings.

It is the goodness of God that allows His children to enter the fiery furnace and the lions' den. It is the goodness of God that allows men to serve Him in weakness and to carry "thorns" in their flesh.

That individual who looks upon God as a sadist because He allows His children to suffer needs to take a second look at Calvary. He needs a new relationship with the "Man of Sorrows" Who was acquainted with grief and afflicted.

Sickness, sorrow, suffering, and even death (John 11:4) can be for the glory of God. He who misses this truth misses one of the great principles of Scripture and lays himself open to delusion and broken fellowship with God.

But what about those who claim that healing is in the atonement? With this as the basis, they argue that it is never the will of God for a Christian to be ill. Such teaching cannot be substantiated by Scripture. On several occasions in the New Testament we are introduced to servants of the Lord who were sick, i.e., Paul, Timothy, and Trophimus. Church history bears witness to the fact that some of the finest servants and saints of the Lord have suffered days, months, and even years of pain.

There is, of course, an element of truth concerning healing in the atonement, but it must be considered in its proper setting. Let me illustrate. The "new heavens and new earth" are in the atonement (II Peter 3:13), but their time is not yet. The changing of our "vile body" into the likeness of His glorious body is in the atonement, but it must await the appearing of Christ (Phil. 3:20-21). We are now the sons of God, but we are not yet what we will be (I John 3:2).

Though the atonement makes provision for physical and spiritual perfection, that perfection will not be realized until we are like Him. This will take place when we see Him as He is.

He who believes it is never in the will of God for a child of God to be sick must of necessity believe that when the child of God is sick he is out of the will of God. Neither the Bible nor experience confirms this view. On the contrary the Scriptures teach that there is a significant relationship between suffering and the growth of the soul.

How important a place suffering played in the lives of Old Testament heroes of the faith. They were scourged, imprisoned, stoned, sawn asunder, afflicted, tormented, and slain with the sword (Heb. 11). In the New Testament, Paul was beaten with thirty-nine stripes on five occasions. He was three times beaten with rods, stoned once, and shipwrecked three times (II Cor. 11:23-24). Many of the believers at Jerusalem, Corinth, and Thessalonica knew what it meant to suffer for Christ.

But is there not a difference between sickness

and the suffering experienced by those we have just mentioned? Yes and no! The end result of being born blind, or being blinded as a result of a brain injury from an unavoidable accident, or being blinded by an enemy of the Gospel who gouged out the eyes is the same. In all likelihood the suffering person was not out of the will of God in any of these cases.

If sickness and suffering have no place in the will of God for our lives, those saints of old who were tortured and afflicted apparently didn't know this truth and thus made a big mistake in not claiming deliverance and healing. Paul then blundered seriously in glorying in his infirmities.

In order to believe that sickness is never to have any place in the body of the child of God, it is necessary to believe that this mortal has already put on immortality and this corruptible has put on incorruption (I Cor. 15:52-54). On the contrary, we are still in mortal bodies which are subject to decay and death. Though immortality is in the atonement, we will not enter into it in its fullness until the trump of God sounds and we are raised incorruptible. As long as we are in the flesh we are subject to weakness, infirmity, sickness, and death. Though the atonement has provided for a day in which all tears, sorrow, and suffering will be wiped away, that day is still future.

In order to be consistent in one's faith that it is never the will of God for one to be sick, it is necessary to believe in sinless perfection. If one could somehow eradicate all the results of sin from the human body, he would be in a position where weakness, infirmities, and decay could not touch him. You will note that he would not simply have to live apart from acts of sin but rid himself of the fact of sin. It would actually be necessary for him to deliver himself from his Adamic nature and from this body of humiliation, so subject to infirmities and decay.

There is no illustration of sinless perfection among the children of God in the New Testament. Furthermore, even though the Son of God lived a sinless life, it was because He took upon Himself the form of man (a human body) that He was able to suffer in the flesh for us. He could not have suffered for us in His pre-incarnation form. Nor could He have suffered in His post-resurrection, glorified body. In other words, there is a relationship between mortal bodies and suffering, sickness, decay, and death. As long as man is of the earth earthy, his body will be subject to these things (I Cor. 15).

Grace and strength to live in the face of these facts, along with the glorious, purifying hope of ultimate deliverance and victory provide the Christian answer to the fact that we live in a suffering world. Romans 8:37-39 sounds forth this note of triumph: "Nay, in all these things we are more than conquerors through him that loved us. For I am persuaded, that neither death, nor life, nor angels, nor principalities, nor powers, nor things present, nor things to come, nor height, nor depth, nor any other creature, shall be able to separate us from the love of God, which is in Christ Jesus our Lord."

18

SOME CONCLUDING OBSERVATIONS

TO WHAT CONCLUSION has all our study led us? May we now declare that we have said the last word on healing — that we are *the* authority on the subject? Perhaps not, but at least we are in a good position to consider some general observations which will in turn become guidelines enabling us to objectively evaluate various "healing" situations when we face them.

The first generalization is that we are apparently in the midst of a revival of healing ministries. Like history itself, certain religious truths repeat themselves. Interest in them rises and falls in varying degrees of intensity. This is even true of such fundamental doctrines as the authority of the Scriptures, the deity of the Son of God, and the return of Christ. How much more it is true of those teachings which touch the bodies and emotions of people.

Nor can one deny that economic and sociological conditions affect these religious trends. Prosperity has a tendency to cause men to forget God. War, famine, earthquake, and pestilence turn men's thoughts in the direction of a supreme Being. Then prophecy takes on new significance in the pronouncements of the church. Times of tension, strain, frustration, and "cold wars" magnify the importance of healing, health, rest, and peace. Beyond question the tensions in which man finds himself today have contributed largely to the increased interest in healing ministries.

Old-line denominations are giving new attention to the subject of spiritual healing. They are making a calculated attempt to discover its place within the framework of the church. Sermons on the subject are being preached, pamphlets and books written, and healing missions held.

Dr. R. B. Bell, founder of the Life Abundant Movement, says, "We are at last beginning to understand that healing of the sick is a must in Christian obligation." Emily Gardiner Neal says, "My wonder is not that there should be resurgence of spiritual healing in the middle of the twentieth century, . . . but that every church in Christendom has not already incorporated it into its active spiritual life" *(A Reporter Finds God Through Spiritual Healing,* p. 89). Mrs. Neal declares, "Today's miracles of healing, both spiritual and physical, signify the greatest revival of spiritual power the church has known since apostolic days."

This revival of spiritual healing which is taking place within old-line denominations is quite apart from the large healing campaigns carried on by professional healers. When one considers the use of radio and television it is safe to say that the "professionals" have a greater outreach and influence than ever before.

Our second generalization is that healings have taken place in the past and are taking place in the present. Some of these healings take place under circumstances which are contrary to

Scriptural teaching, while others fit squarely into the Biblical pattern.

An estimated three million pilgrims journey to Lourdes, France, every year. It is claimed that about 2 percent of those seeking healing at the Lourdes shrine receive it. The Lourdes Medical Commission has accepted as miracles about fifty cases from among the many thousands who have claimed healing. It is not the purpose of this booklet to explain the healings which may take place at Catholic shrines. It is simply to report the claims in order that the reader might realize their existence.

Christian Science has documented hundreds of healings in the past, and continues to do so in the present. Again, the question as to whether these "healings" are the result of mind over matter, interventions of God, or the work of Satan is not the basic issue in this book. The fact is, certain types of illnesses are apparently healed within the context of Christian Science teaching. As far as this writer can ascertain, neither the Catholic shrine nor Christian Science healings fit into the Biblical pattern.

How about "professional" healing campaigns? Are there genuine restorations to health that come about as a result of hands placed on the radio or television while a "divine healer" prays? Are men and women who go forward in the healing lines or find their way to the healing rooms in these campaigns healed? The answer is, "Yes, some of them."

Can it also be said that the sick are healed in nonprofessional healing services in which they come forward in church to be prayed for? Again we feel the answer is "Yes." This same response applies to the hospital room or the sickbed at home to which some pastor or believing friends have been called for prayer.

Yes, healings are taking place. Some of them through Satanic forces. A far greater percentage through the power of mind over matter. Some result from a form of hypnotism or the power of suggestion. Others are psychosomatically induced. Others are the result of casting one's care upon the Lord and resting in His goodness. Yet others are the direct result of believing prayer. The latter are miraculous demonstrations of the intervention of God in the realm of physical well-being.

However, it is noteworthy that none of these generalizations have anything to do with the "gifts of healing." Though some of them may have some relationship with James 5, they are all outside the realm of I Corinthians 12. If there is anyone on earth today who has the "gifts of healing," this writer has neither met him nor read of him. He has read of those who appear to demonstrate the "gifts of healing," but he is unable to fit those demonstrations into the framework of Bible teaching. The ministry of professional healers does not coincide with either the acts or the attitudes of those who exercised the gifts of healing in the early church.

There is no doubt that God answers the prayers of His believing children and works miracles of healing when it is for His glory. There are genuine and undeniable cases of miraculous restoration to health which can only be accounted for on the basis of the power of God. They, however, are not commonplace. They are the exception rather than the rule. There are thousands of suffering saints who bear witness to this fact. But they believe in and rejoice in Romans 8:28-29: "And we know that all things work together for good to them that love God, to them who are the called according to his purpose. For whom he did foreknow, he also did predestinate to be conformed to the image of his Son, that he might be the firstborn among many brethren."